D0132576

# THE ART OF BREAKING UP

## THE HEARTBREAKER SIDE

The following pages include artwork, poetry,
short stories, games, and illustrations made
collaboratively on HITRECORD.org—an online creative
platform with a community of more than 750,000
artists from around the world.

This side alone features 538 contributions
from 228 unique artists.

To learn more about this production and how this
book was made, or to contribute your own stories
and artwork to ongoing challenges, visit
*www.hitrecord.org/artofbreakingup*.

HarperCollins books may be purchased for educational, business,
or sales promotional use. For information please email the
Special Markets Department at SPsales@harpercollins.com.

First published in 2020 by
Harper Design
An Imprint of HarperCollinsPublishers
195 Broadway
New York, NY 10007
Tel: (212) 207-7000
Fax: (855) 746-6023
harperdesign@harpercollins.com
www.hc.com

Distributed throughout North America by
HarperCollinsPublishers
195 Broadway
New York, NY 10007
ISBN 978-0-06-289649-0
Library of Congress Control Number: 2018965717
Printed in China
First Printing, 2020
www.hitrecord.org

Dear Reader:

Welcome to the HEARTBREAKER side of the book. What you are about to read is an ode to a human experience that most everyone—man or woman, gay or straight, rich or poor, crazy or sane, Capulet or Montague—can relate to. Yes, friend, we are referring to breaking up with someone.

It isn't easy to let someone go (unless you're Rose from *Titanic* who let Jack go to the bottom of the ocean, EVEN THOUGH LET'S FACE IT, THERE WAS ROOM ON THAT FLOATING PIECE OF WOOD FOR THE BOTH OF THEM.)

But sometimes, that special someone turns into that not-so-special someone.

Things about them that used to make you smile begin to make you grimace. Their immaturity, sloppiness, or adultery have become too much to handle and somewhere along the way became the very straw that broke the camel's back. So one day you take the only option you see fit: You dump their ass. Congratulations. Time to give yourself a well-deserved pat on the back, you heartbreaker, you.

We don't blame you, and neither do the hundreds of people who filled the following pages with their unique experiences about breaking hearts and taking names. The writing and artwork within these pages is the result of a collaborative effort between heartbreakers all over the world. So, friend, we encourage you to read this book, stare at it blankly, keep it in your bathroom for light reading/emergency TP, or use it as a weapon for self-defense when your psychotic ex disobeys that restraining order. This is *The Art of Breaking Up*—the HEARTBREAKER side.

With Severed Love,
Your Fellow Heartbreakers


P.S. Maybe you've never broken up with someone—you've always been on the receiving end. If that's the case, it may do you some good to flip through these pages and get a real glimpse into the mind of a manipulative love genius. You might even get closure, or at the very least, fill in some of the blanks as to why you're always being taken out with the trash. xoxo.

# CONTENTS

The psychological stages of healing outline the phases that someone who is grief stricken—or BROKEN HEARTED—undergoes. But what if there was nothing to grieve? What happens to the person who does the breaking up?

See how the healing process plays out in reverse for the HEARTBREAKER by flipping through these pages and getting a front-row seat to the deterioration of a relationship, its celebratory end, and the unintended aftereffects.

# 1
# EARLY WARNING SIGNS

Ah, relationships: the stability, the commitment, the boredom. There was a time when you found their quirks and habits adorable, but now...not so much.

**This is the EARLY WARNING SIGNS chapter**—or the art of suddenly hating everything you once found charming about your partner.

# EARLY WARNING SIGNS QUIZ

MOOD SWINGS

1. **When your partner starts telling you about their day, you:**

   A. Listen attentively. You just can't get over the appeal of the dulcet tone of their voice.

   B. Listen halfheartedly while mentally planning what you will watch on TV later that night.

   C. Look around the room for something to stab yourself in the eye with.

   D. Look around the room for something to stab your partner in the eye with.

2. **When you make love, you:**

   A. Participate 100 percent with your mind, body, and soul. You both have such a good connection.

   B. Participate with your body and imagine your partner is someone else.

   C. Participate by getting really drunk first and imagine you're someone else.

   D. Participate with anyone but your partner.

3. **When you listen to the sounds of your partner eating, you imagine:**

   A. A cute little guinea pig chewing on a carrot.

   B. Your slightly overweight cat who acts like every feeding time may be the last.

   C. Pigs rolling around in mud and in their own feces while a farmer pitches a bucket of slop into a trough.

   D. This is what Dante's underreported tenth circle of hell must be like.

4. **The thought of being apart from your partner for a significant amount of time makes you:**

   A. Feel sad. You post messages all over social media telling them how much you miss them.

   B. Feel a little melancholic, perhaps, but confident that some time apart will make you appreciate them all the more.

   C. Feel like you won the lottery. How soon can they leave?

   D. Relieved! You smile and feel all warm inside.

5.  **When your partner makes plans for the both of you without your knowledge, you:**

    A. Are so excited! They know how much you love surprises! You can't wait to find out what new adventure awaits you.

    B. Prepare to give it a go but just hope you can compromise if it's something you really don't want to do.

    C. Go with them but spend the entire time either silent or being passive-aggressive about everything.

    D. Scream like a spoiled child, "You're not the boss of me! You can't tell me what to do!" and lock yourself in the bathroom.

6.  **You're going on vacation together. The first thing you want to do is:**

    A. Hang the "Do not disturb" sign on the door and don't leave the room for a day.

    B. Shower and head to the pool; you expect compliments on how hot you look in your new swimwear.

    C. Make friends with fellow vacationers so you don't have to spend a week talking to your partner.

    D. Tip off airport security when you land that your partner is smuggling something they shouldn't be. *Hasta mañana sucker.*

## Results

For every **A** reply, give yourself **5 points**.

For every **B** reply, give yourself **10 points**.

For every **C** reply, give yourself **15 points**.

For every **D** reply, give yourself **20 points**.

**30-40 points:** There are no warning signs to watch out for because you are happy and in love. Your relationship is still in the honeymoon stage. Stay with this person because they make you happy and satisfied.

**40-65 points:** You are happy, but there are little warning signs that you could probably spend some time working through small issues with each other before they turn into anything bigger.

**65-90 points:** There could be trouble ahead. Try taking a little time apart to reflect on your relationship. Look for areas where there could be issues, and strive to work on them together. Consider whether you are both putting the work into this partnership and whether you still want to be in it.

**90-120 points:** You don't have to be a rocket scientist to figure this one out, do you? Well in case you do...there are warning signs the size of Texas that this relationship is doomed. Get out while you can. There is no coming back from this. It's as dead as a dodo.

ROUNDABOUT
EXPLANATION
AHEAD

# THE PROS & CON OF SPLITTING UP

## The Pros

-I won't get nagged if I don't load the dishwasher as if I were playing *Tetris*.

-I never have to share a Twix again.

-I can lick the spoon and put it back in the jar of Nutella.

-MUCH more room to sit in the closet and eat ice cream.

-No need to brush my teeth EVERY day.

-Farting!

-I never have to pretend that I haven't fallen asleep watching some crappy movie.

-The return of Masturbation Mondays, Tug It Tuesdays, Wank Daft Wednesdays, and the introduction of Two Fingers Thursdays.

-Chillin' on the weekend. EVERY weekend.

## The Con

-Silence :(

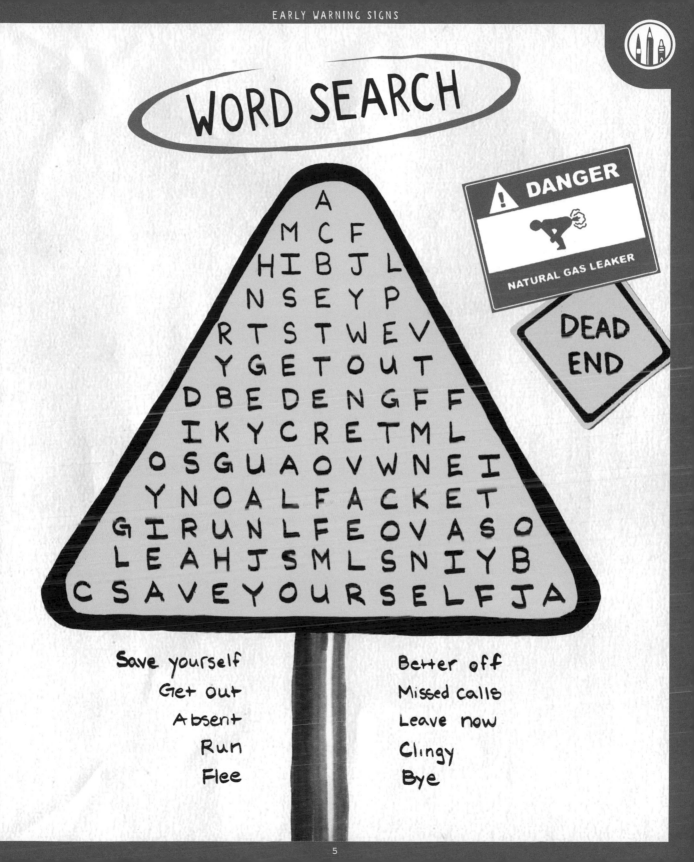

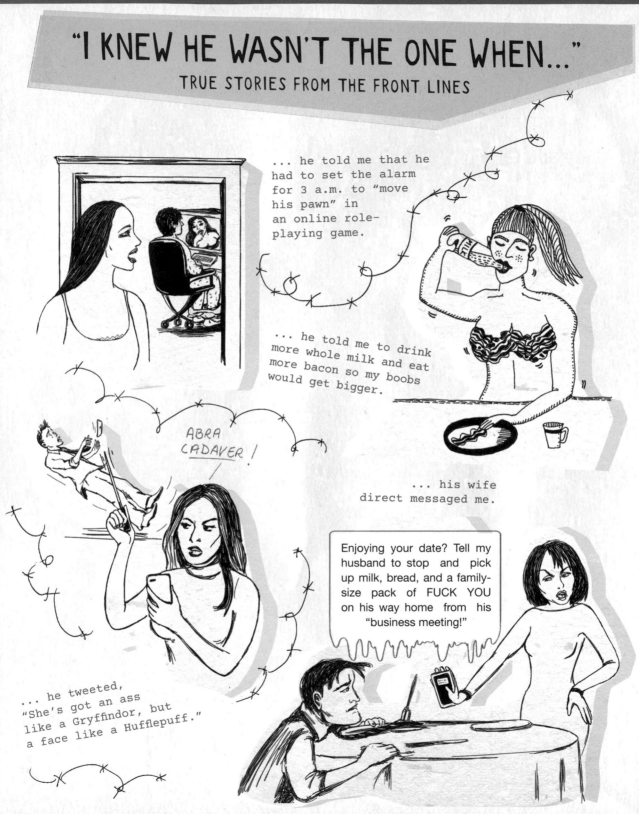

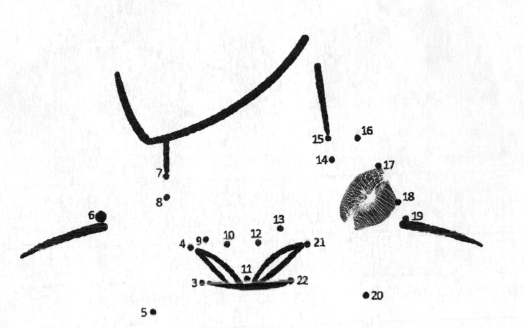

15• 16•

14• 17•

7• 18•

8• 6• 13• 19•

10 12

4• 9• 11 21

3• 22

20•

5•

2• 23•

1•

•24

# Connect the dots

# PHOTOGRAPHIC EVIDENCE

OUR HEARTBREAKER—THE PLAINTIFF—WAS BUILDING A STRONG CASE AGAINST HER SOON-TO-BE EX-HUSBAND. THE EVIDENCE WAS OVERWHELMING. HERE'S WHAT CONVICTED HIM IN THE COURT OF HER MIND:

Defendant insisted that the plaintiff leave their joint-owned condominium whenever he had to "go number two."

Defendant refused to inform his parents of marriage to the plaintiff for a period of no less than twelve months following said ceremony.

Defendant's parents were speechless.

Following the plaintiff suffering a broken pelvis, the defendant repeatedly—and insensitively—inquired as to when they could resume intercourse.

Defendant only booked one first-class ticket for their joint vacation.

On numerous occasions, the defendant compared the plaintiff to his sister, specifically "in the looks department."

# WARNING SIGNS AT EVERY AGE

SPEED BUMPS AHEAD

Breakups can happen at any stage of life. Take a look at this list of carefully curated warning signs by our world-renowned group of breakup specialists.

**Age 3:** They do not share their LEGOs.

**Age 7:** They would rather eat mud than hold your hand.

**Age 16:** They are texting your BFF more than you.

**Age 22:** They hang from the ledge of a twenty-story building to take a selfie, but they refuse to drive twenty minutes to meet your parents because it's raining.

**Age 27:** They plan date nights by creating an "event" on social media and then marking it as a "maybe."

**Age 31:** They tell you how much you remind them of their mother.

**Age 35:** They eat pizza over their tax forms...at their parents' house...where they still live.

**Age 41:** They create a dating app profile "as a joke" and then keep updating their pics and bio.

**Age 46:** They keep referring to their three children but you only have two together.

**Age 51:** They buy you a vacuum cleaner for your birthday.

No TURNING BACK

**Age 62:** They keep making "jokes" about the "Swinging Sixties."

**Age 72:** They sign up for a seniors' cruise and deny they knew it was for singles only.

**Age 81:** They steal the best pudding cups from the buffet and hoard them without telling you.

**Age 90:** They refuse to consider adjacent cemetery plots, feigning concern for the legal repercussions of breaking the "'til death do us part" clause in your marriage contract.

# 2
# EXIT STRATEGY

You know you've got to end it, but now you have to figure out how. Should you let them down gently, or should you twist the knife?

**This is the EXIT STRATEGY chapter**—or the art of planning your escape in a way that minimizes the pain...to yourself, at least.

# THE REHEARSAL

# EXITING THE ESCAPE ROOM

GAME over

Need to make a swift escape? Follow this stealthy plan to retrieve all of your belongings without leaving a trace!

A
FINDING CLUES FROM BROKEN MEMORABILIA

B
HINT: Anniversary
HACK INTO PHONE TO DELETE SHARED STREAMING ACCOUNT

C
BURN PLANT TO RETRIEVE KEYS

D
RETRIEVING and REUNITING LONG LOST SOCK

E
UNPAIR COUPLE STUFF

DRAW YOUR IDEAL GETAWAY VEHICLE

GET OFF AT NEXT EX

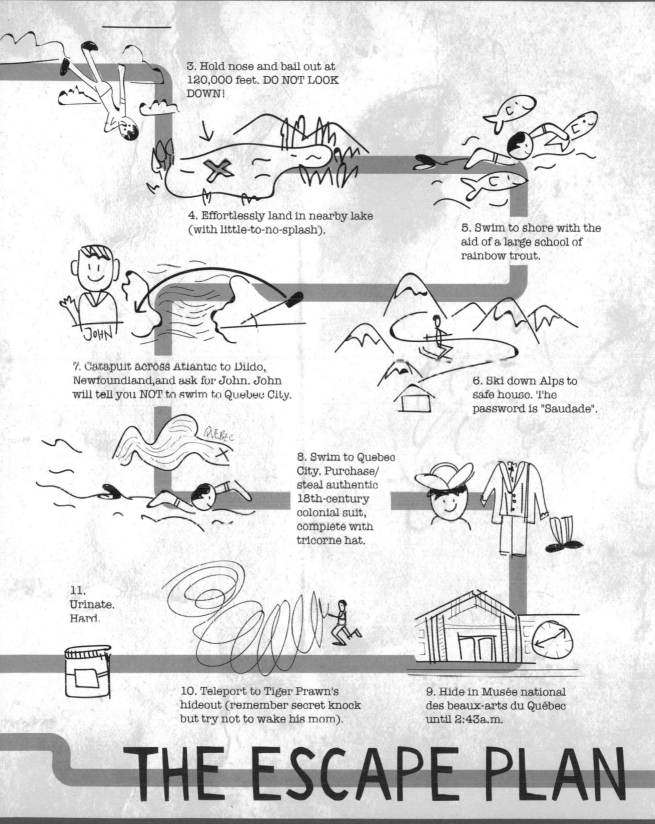

3. Hold nose and bail out at 120,000 feet. DO NOT LOOK DOWN!

4. Effortlessly land in nearby lake (with little-to-no-splash).

5. Swim to shore with the aid of a large school of rainbow trout.

7. Catapult across Atlantic to Dildo, Newfoundland, and ask for John. John will tell you NOT to swim to Quebec City.

6. Ski down Alps to safe house. The password is "Saudade".

8. Swim to Quebec City. Purchase/steal authentic 18th-century colonial suit, complete with tricorne hat.

11. Urinate. Hard.

10. Teleport to Tiger Prawn's hideout (remember secret knock but try not to wake his mom).

9. Hide in Musée national des beaux-arts du Québec until 2:43a.m.

# THE ESCAPE PLAN

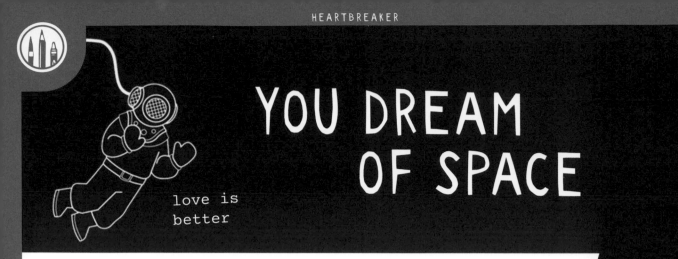

# YOU DREAM OF SPACE

love is
better

WHAT ARE YOU GOING TO DO WITH ALL OF IT?!
WRITE OR DRAW YOUR PLAN IN THE SPACE BELOW...

from a
distance

# HAIKU

IF I PACK MY STUFF
AND SNEAK OUT WHILE YOU'RE SLEEPING
WILL YOU HATE ME MORE?

IS IT RUDE TO TEXT?
EMOJIS WILL LAY THE GROUND
FOR MY GETAWAY

I'd have more success
By faking my own death, dear
So please leave me now

YOU PAINTED PICTURES
OF HOW YOU THOUGHT I SHOULD BE
BUT NEVER OF ME

I REALLY LOVED YOU
BUT IT SEEMS YOU'LL NEVER LEARN
TOILET SEAT STAYS DOWN

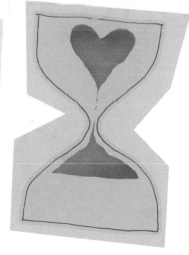

# HEALTH AND SAFETY GUIDE

## BEFORE THE BREAKUP

*We all know that breakups can get messy...even hazardous. When you find yourself in a risky situation, it is of utmost importance to prepare yourself physically, sexually, spiritually, and, yes, emotionally. The following health and safety tips will ensure that you take the necessary precautions leading up to the relationship extraction point.*

**Before the Breakup**

**1)** If you are reliant on your partner for health insurance, get a thorough examination well in advance. Make sure your vaccinations are up to date, your prescriptions are filled, and your mental stability is confirmed (in writing). This may come in handy if your partner should accuse you of being sick and/or deranged. If you uncover any pre-existing conditions, consider delaying the breakup until after you've received any necessary treatment.

   **Bonus Tip:** This would be an ideal time to update your "In Case of Emergency" contact info!

**2)** Lay claim to the mutual friends you want to keep by giving them thoughtful, impromptu gifts. Plant seeds of doubt by saying things like, "I don't know why X always says you're boring. I have tons of fun with you!" They'll be on your side before it's even time to choose.

   **3)** Decide on a date for the Big Day! Make sure it's not a holiday or anyone's birthday or anniversary. Or, do...if you really want to be a dick about it.

   **4)** Take inventory of all your valuables, including but not limited to: photographs, clothing, glass menageries, potential weapons, etc. Store them for safekeeping. Do the same with your partner's valuables. Should things go south, you'll be able to sell their stuff for a substantial profit later.

   **5)** The night before the Big Day, get a good night's sleep! There's no telling how the breakup will go, and you'll need to have your wits about you. And besides, you may find yourself sleeping with one eye open after tomorrow.

# ONE-ROUTE-OUT MAZE

# BREAKUP FORTUNE TELLER

## HOW TO PLAY

1. Follow the folding instructions to make the Breakup Fortune Teller.
2. Ask your soon-to-be ex to pick a colored quadrant. Move the Fortune Teller once for every letter in the color's name (4x for blue, 3x for red, etc.).
3. Ask your soon-to-be ex's lucky number and move the Fortune Teller back and forth that many times.
4. Reveal the breakup message on the inside flap and read it out loud to your soon-to-be ex.

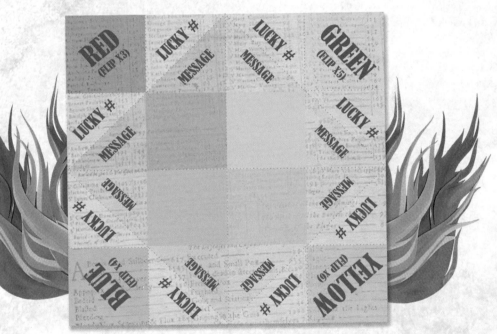

## SAMPLE BREAKUP MESSAGES

**- DIRECT -**
Let's split up.
There's the door.
I don't love you.
G2G.

**- ANGRY -**
We are done!!!
Fuck off!!!

Game over.

**- EUPHEMISM -**
Let's find even better halves.
You stole my heart, I want it back.
I hate scheduling, let's not do it ever.

# FOLDING INSTRUCTIONS

**1.**

Take your soon-to-be ex's latest credit card statement and turn the first page into a square. Dispose of the other seven pages.

**2.**

Fold it into a triangle with the balance facing out. (You want to maintain your anger levels.)

**3.**

Fold it again to hide all the consecutive underwear purchases.

**4.**

Unfold the square and remind yourself that you will NEVER have to pay those bills again.

**5.**

Fold the corners to meet the center and think about how you'll never have to make your bed, EVER again.

**6.**

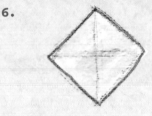

Flip the new square over. At least something in your life allows you to experiment with a backside.

**7.**

Fold the corners to meet the center again. Seriously, what's the point of making your bed if you're just going to mess it up again?

**8.**

Number the sections from 1-8. For every number you write, imagine a peaceful hour of un-spooned sleep.

**9.**

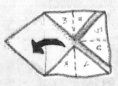

Open the flaps and write a personalized breakup message on each one. This is where you tell them you're opening a bank account on your own, by the way.

# 3
# THE BREAKUP

This is it. The main event. But try not to drag it out. Think of it like taking off a band-aid...a band-aid that's covering a shot-gun wound to the chest.

**This is, THE BREAKUP chapter**—or the art of attempting open heart surgery with no medical training.

# THE HIDDEN MESSAGE MIXTAPE

The Beatles - *Oh! Darling*

Beyoncé - *Sorry*

ELO - *It's Over*

Pink Floyd - *If*

R.E.M. - *You*

The Smiths - *Where Did Our Love Go?*

Bill Withers - *I Don't Know*

Adele - *All I Ask*

James Brown - *Please, Please, Please*

Elvis Presley - *Don't*

Blondie - *Call Me*

Ed Sheeran - *Don't*

Sam Cooke - *You Send Me*

Crosby, Stills & Nash - *Anything At All*

Radiohead - *Just*

Michael Jackson - *Leave Me Alone*

The Beatles - *Because*

Bob Dylan - *It's All Over Now, Baby Blue*

# BREAKUP GAME NIGHT

Breaking up with someone can be SUPER AWKWARD, so why not alleviate the strain by doing the deed during a game night?

## CHRONOLOGICAL CHARADES
Act out your full relationship, your first fight, and every annoying thing the other person has ever done that has led you to this moment.

## OPERATION BREAKUP
The game is just like the classic, except the heart is missing. Along with the funny bone. And spine. And dignity.

## PIN THE BLAME ON THE RELATIONSHIP
Take turns pinpointing the exact reason the relationship failed.

## CHEATERS CLUE
Was it Jane with the maid's outfit on the kitchen table or John with the blue dildo in the back passage?

## BATTLE (RELATION)SHIP
It's sink or swim! Time to rock the boat and torpedo your relationship to oblivion.

## BUGGER OFF BOGGLE
The mind boggles as to why you let this relationship go on for so long. Find the right words to break it up!

## SCREW YOUR SCRABBLE
Phrases are allowed in this version of the popular classic as long as they successfully get the message across. LEAVENOW—Triple Word Score!

A breakup just doesn't change a person—it changes their surroundings. A home can go from a love-filled nest to a loveless mess. Can you see the difference?

before

after

before

after

# WHO GETS WHAT?
## THE BOARD GAME

**Introduction:**
Two players compete for ownership of the most precious items from their relationship by claiming territory on the map of their lives. Battle to claim anything from circles of friends and local hotspots, to treasured possessions and adored pets. Will you break your ex's heart or claim the moral high ground? Channel all your bitterness and anger into *Who Gets What?*

To win, claim the moral high ground or win the breakup by escaping Breakup Island with the most stuff.

**Players:** 2

**Duration:**
Less than a lifetime of unhappiness

**Contents:**
1   Game Board
2   Colored Pencils
1   Eraser
2   Dice (1 D12 and 1 D6)
50  Emotional Blackmail Cards

**Game Setup:**
1)   Put your differences aside for one brief moment.
2)   Using the game board on the right as a reference, draw your own *Who Gets What?* map. Grab some note cards and write out the cards outlined on the right page.
3)   Give each player a colored pencil. Leave the eraser and dice in a convenient, mutually accessible location to avoid additional arguments and throwing of items.
4)   Shuffle the Emotional Blackmail deck and place facedown on the board.

**Playing the Game:**
The person who initiated the breakup plays first.

<u>On your turn:</u>
1) Stare your opponent in the eye—but with more venom than you would at a candlelit dinner—and roll both die.
2) D12 indicates the number of seconds you have to color on the map. Frantically color in blank sections of the map to claim ownership of territories until you run out of time.
3) D6 indicates how long you have to erase your ex's color from the board. When time is up, argue over timekeeping before begrudgingly passing control over to your ex.
4) When you roll doubles you must draw one card from the Emotional Blackmail pile. Perform the action, as described on the card, taking every opportunity to make your opponent fully aware of the emotional impact of the wasted years spent in their company.

**Game End:**
The game ends when the map is fully colored in or neither player can take it anymore. Moral high ground is claimed by the first to walk away from the board. There are no winners, just two individuals keeping different items that once mattered to them but that now feel like someone else's trash. Pack the game away and go on to enjoy your individual lives.

**Game Variation:**
<u>You Get That!:</u> Each player claims territory for the other player, coloring in territories that they don't care about.

## The Emotional Blackmail Cards

<u>The Mother-in-Law card (1):</u> Your self-righteous mother-in-law tells you that you are an asshole and not good enough for her child. Your ex can color for 5 seconds on any area of their choosing.

<u>The Mother-in-Law card (2):</u> Your mother-in-law agrees that the breakup is her child's fault. Immediately claim the TV.

<u>The Father-in-Law card (1):</u> Remind your ex that their father never believed they were responsible enough to have a dog in the first place. Immediately claim The Dog Island.

<u>The Father-in-Law card (2):</u> Your father-in-law doesn't have an opinion. Skip this turn.

<u>Mutual Friends card (1):</u> Remind your ex of the time they got drunk at a friend's wedding. Claim the Single Malt Whiskey.

<u>Mutual Friends card (2):</u> Inform your ex that your friends always thought they were stuck-up, and don't want to attend the Coachella festival this year. Color for 5 seconds on the Local Café.

<u>Pet card:</u> You prove to your ex that the cat prefers you, as she doesn't scratch you when you wake her. Color for 5 seconds on any area of your choosing.

<u>The "Family First" card:</u> Each player names their partner's cousins. Whoever can recall the most names wins and can claim an island of their choosing.

<u>Perfect Meet-up card:</u> You bump into your ex while out with your superhot new pet-sitter. Claim one island of your choosing.

<u>Awkward Encounter card:</u> You run into your ex's BFF while buying ice cream and vodka in your pj's. Immediately forfeit the game.

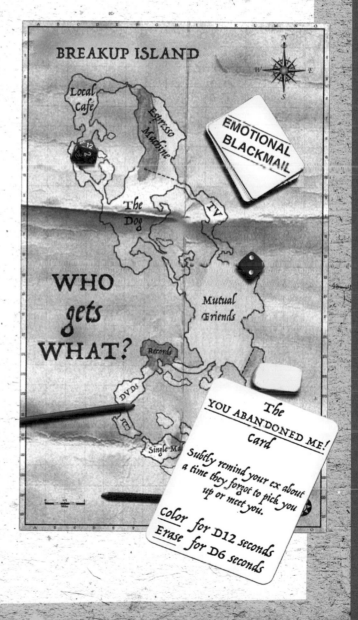

# BREAK UP WITH A CARD

If you want to break up with your significant other but struggle to find the right words, let a card say what you can't! Send your soon-to-be ex a crafty pre-written note that will give you all the perks of a breakup with none of the annoying face-to-face interaction!

You hold the keys....

SingleClub
Cards

Say
it with
a card

I'm lucky in having found the
PuRRfect
PARTNER
to spend my life with...

But the locks have changed.

Surprise!

IT'S **NOT** YOU.

# MY LAST BREAKUP

## A TRUE SHORT STORY

My last breakup before I met my husband stands out in my mind. Partly because I loved him. Partly because his emotional abuse had me all messed up. Mostly because it was my last.

He drank. And when he drank he was mean. It should have been easy to cut him loose, but it wasn't. He told me he was the best thing I would ever have. He told me I would never find anyone to love me like he did. He told me I would be alone.

I believed him.

Until I ended up with a dislocated jaw. The dentist asked if I clenched my teeth? I assured him that I didn't, and together we wondered at the mystery of what caused my injury. I went home. He was there, drinking, and feeling mean. I tried to ignore his words. I clenched and pain shot through my face. I wondered when I had become a woman who broke her own jaw to hold in her words. He was still talking, lips moving, words slurred. I walked across the room and slapped him so hard I drew blood.

The next day I left.

He begged me to stay. He called late at night, he banged on my door yelling that he loved me, waking my neighbors. He offered me gifts and spat venomous words with the same breath. He reminded me I would be alone. That was OK with me.

Being alone was better than being with him.

Eventually, I heard he had a wife and baby. I had my own new baby at the time. I knew how hard it could be and how much I needed the support of my husband. I couldn't imagine being vulnerable with only a mean drunk by my side. I wanted to rescue her—this poor woman that had become his wife. I imagined showing up at the door, telling her I knew how lonely and empty life could be with him. I imagined telling her it didn't have to be that way.

I didn't do that, of course. But every now and then—when I remember what it was like to live with him, and how it felt coming back to life after I left—I wish that I had saved her, or at least tried.

THEY SAY FRENCH IS THE LANGUAGE OF LOVE...
BUT IT'S USELESS FOR BREAKING UP.

HERE'S A HANDY LANGUAGE GUIDE SO YOU CAN BREAK
UP WITH PANACHE:

## GERMAN

| ORIGINAL | TRANSLATION |
| --- | --- |
| Hau ab! | Fuck off! |
| Zisch ab! | Whoosh away! |
| Verpiss dich! | Piss off! |

### SPICE IT UP!

| | |
| --- | --- |
| Angsthase | Frightened rabbit |
| Hosenscheisser | Pants-shitter |
| Lustmolch | Lust newt |
| Muttersöhnchen | Mother's son |
| Ochsenschädel | Ox skull |
| Schlappschwanz | Floppy tail |
| Schnapsdrossel | Booze thrush |
| Arschgesicht | Ass face |
| Hackfresse | Ground-meat face |

## DUTCH

| ORIGINAL | TRANSLATION |
| --- | --- |
| Opzouten! | Salt up! |
| Ga fietsen! | Go ride your bike! |
| Scheer je weg! | Shave away! |

### SPICE IT UP!

| | |
| --- | --- |
| Eikel | Acorn/top of penis |
| Klottzak | Scrotum |
| Lul | Penis |
| Dikzak | Fat scrotum |
| Rund | Cow |
| Hondelul | Dog dick |
| Lul de behanger | Penis the wall paperer |
| Schijtluis | Shitting lice |
| Oen | Castrated donkey |
| Mierenneuker | Ant fucker |
| Hou je bek! | Keep your animal mouth |
| Uilskuiken | Baby owl |
| Zakkenwasser | Washer of bag/scrotum washer |

## BINARY

| 011 111 0010 0011  11 0010  010 00 101 1110 0 00 0100  110 0000 10 | "You have a limp hard drive" |
| --- | --- |

AND OF COURSE, THE PERENNIAL: IT'S NOT YOU, IT'S ME.

**JAPANESE:** あなたのせいじゃない。わたしのせい。
(Pronunciation: Kimi Ja nai yo. Boku da!)

**LATVIAN:** Tā nav tava vaina, tā ir mana.

**SPANISH:** No eres tú, soy yo.

**HEBREW:** Ze lo ata-ze ani.

**IRISH:** Ní ort é, is orm é.

**PIG-LATIN:** It's sway otnay ouyay, it'sway emay.

**ELVISH:** Im mel cin but im'm ú-in mel with cin.

**ERMAHGERD:** Ert's nert yer, ert's mer.

# BITTERLING
## A SHORT STORY

They don't write songs or books or movies about how to be a heartbreaker—at least, not in a serious sense. Sure, there's cutesy stuff, but the perspective so often hinges on the heartbroken, as if breakups are hard only on one half of the relationship. It's incomprehensible that you hurt each and every day. But you are terrified to leave because you'll crush someone you loved. Someone you still love, but not in the same way you once did. So you don't make a decision at all. Things will sort themselves out. Life will continue, a river unperturbed. But inside, you're all ripples, water catching on every jagged nerve.

On date night—scheduled each week on the same day and at the same place you hate—you stare across the table, a steak knife in your left hand. You wonder, which would be worse: slicing their carotid artery or your own. Your fingers tighten around the metal handle until you're nearly shaking.

"Is everything okay?"

No. No, everything isn't okay. You want to scream.

Only you don't scream. You're silent, you gasp for air like a bitterling stranded on the sand. Tears prick the insides of your eyes, but you blink them back down into submission; you refuse to cry over your coconut curry. It's already oversalted. "This tastes like MSG," you say.

"Oh. You want something else?"

You shake your head and stare down at your plate.

Later, you close your eyes as your bodies collide in the same rhythm they do every two to three days (less if you can help it). You very often picture other people—anyone, really—tonight it's Chris Evans, Chris Pine, Chris Pratt, Chris Pratt when he was still a tiny bit fat and who is actually your favorite of them all, the androgynous cashier at Whole Foods, the even more androgynous barista who served you a black eye this morning.

"You. Are. So. Sexy," your partner whispers with each thrust, nearing climax. His muscles tighten and twitch. He holds you tightly to his soggy chest, his heart beating rapidly. "I love you so much," he says. And he means it.

He rolls off you, and you roll onto your side, clutching your pillow. Should you lie, or tell him the truth? And how do you even explain the truth, when you don't even know quite what you feel anymore? The most you can come up with is nothing—you feel nothing. You feel numb. You've traveled from love through hate, and have arrived at indifference. Maybe you could frame it as a joke: So, good news is I don't hate you. Bad news is it's worse than that.

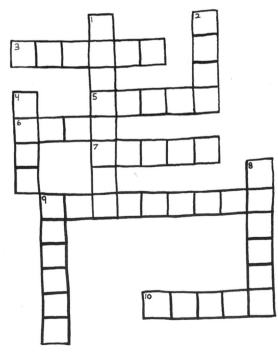

## DOWN

1. Not paying together
2. A job well ____
4. Luke Skywalker's bestie
8. Jordan Peele's directorial debut
9. Make like a ball and ____

## ACROSS

3. Not the beginning
5. Kevin McCallister is *Home* ____
6. The game is done—it's ____
7. Not together
9. N*SYNC's breakup anthem
10. James McAvoy plays multiple personalities

# HEALTH AND SAFETY GUIDE

## DURING THE BREAKUP

*Your relationship has become unhealthy, but your breakup doesn't have to be! Follow these important health and safety tips to ensure yourself a safe, secure, and painless breakup.*

**Breakup Day**

**1)** Eat a substantial meal beforehand. This event could last several hours, and it's considered a breakup faux pas to take a snack break.

**2)** Make sure to use the bathroom ahead of time. Use of a catheter or adult diaper can prevent delays during the event, but to feel like #1, leave the #2 at home.

> **Bonus Tip:** If it's their home and you don't expect to return, feel free to leave the deuce unflushed, as a parting gift.

**3)** Choose a breakup location that exudes a calming, zen feel. Avoid areas with excessive or aggressive noise. If possible, arrange for a public place with plenty of witnesses and, preferably, security equipment in use.

**4)** Arrive early! This will give you the opportunity to: locate all emergency exits and designate an escape route free from obstacles; identify and remove all objects that could be used as makeshift weapons; clear the area of any dangerous/flammable fluids; extinguish any open flames.

# WELCOME
## TO *The Breakup*
# CASINO
## NEVADA

*Breaking up is a gamble. Staying together is a gamble! Here at the HEARTBREAK HOTEL, we can help make this decision easy for you in the comfort of our brand-new luxurious BREAKUP CASINO where each game is specifically designed to determine your future!*

### RELATIONSHIP ROULETTE
Ditch the stress and let the wheel make the decision for you. Stay or leave: place your bets now! Bet on the number of days left before you dump all your soon-to-be-ex's crap on the sidewalk.

### TEXAS HOLD 'EM OR LEAVE 'EM
Our uniquely designed twist on a casino classic allows YOU to take control! Now all the cards are on the table, do you . . .
   A) FOLD your relationship?
   B) CALL your partner and tell them you're sorry?
   C) Go ALL IN and propose marriage?

## Breakup Bonanza

Hit the jackpot with our exclusive one-armed bandit. The odds of hitting the love of your life may be astronomically high, but this slot pays out in fool's gold coins.

## Sweetheart Sweepstakes

Check out all the runners and riders from last year's Sweetheart Sweepstakes, and bet on the one that most closely matches your partner. Should it finish first, not only do you win big, you also get to stay together! WIN-WIN?!

- WIDE BOY: 40/1 "easily distracted"
- FLY-BY-NIGHT: 18/1 "makes all the running, lacks stamina, struggles when going is hard"
- LAME DUCK: 66/1 "showed initial promise but faded badly"
- BIG FLOP: 100/1 "did not finish last time out"
- NO DRAMA: 4/6 Favorite "reliable, stays the course"

# 4
# ACCEPTANCE

Ahh, the sweet, sweet smell of freedom. It's time to spread your wings and see how high you can fly without that pesky ball and chain weighing you down.

**This is the ACCEPTANCE chapter**—or the art of rediscovering the joys of single life.

FREEDOM CHECKLIST:

[ ] GET BETTER SLEEP

[ ] CONTROL THE REMOTE

[ ] NO WEIRD HAIR EVERYWHERE

[X] ORDER WHOLE PIZZA FOR MYSELF

[ ] HOG ENTIRE BLANKET

[ ] CHEW WITH MOUTH OPEN

[X] DANCE NAKED WITH JAR OF
    PEANUT BUTTER AT 2 A.M.

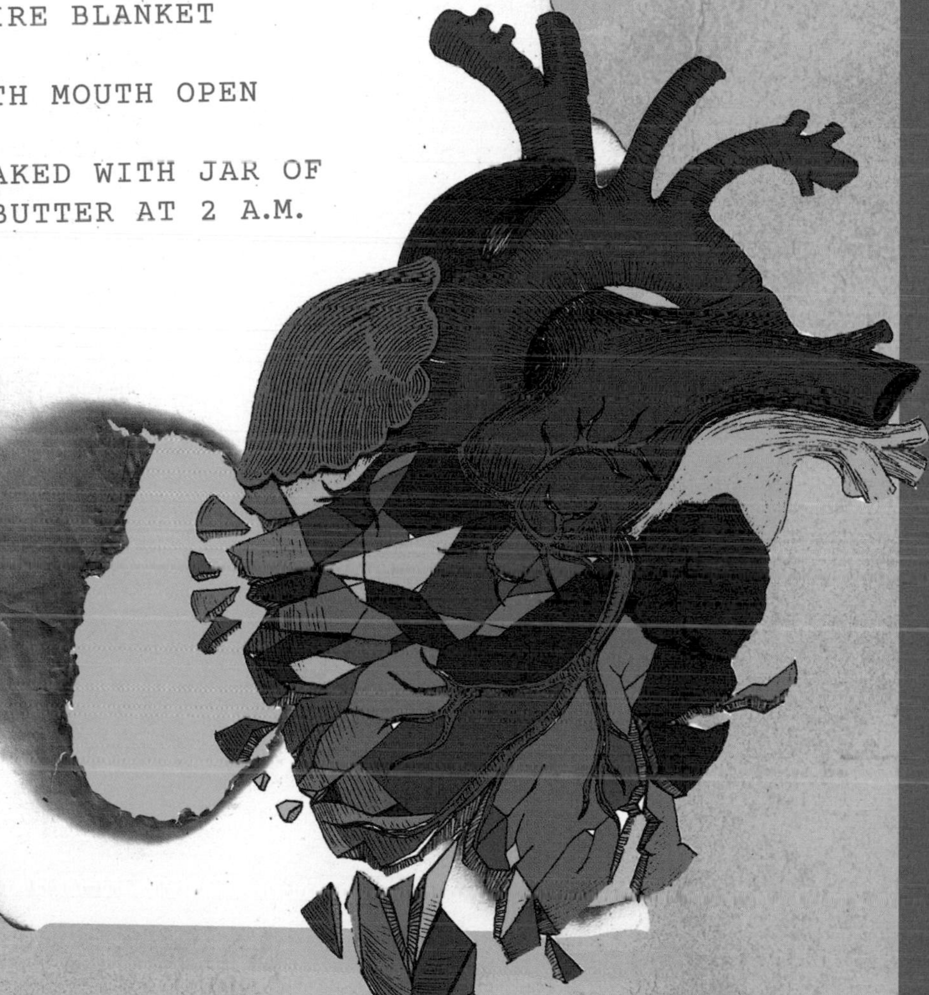

# COLORING PAGE

# HEALTH AND SAFETY GUIDE

## AFTER THE BREAKUP

*You may have survived the disaster, located your nearest exit, and proceeded through the planned evacuation route, but you're not quite in the clear. In order to restore critical functions, manage stabilization, and return to normalcy, follow these important health and safety tips.*

### After the Breakup

**1)** After successfully evacuating the breakup location, take a different route home, checking behind you frequently to ensure you aren't being followed.

**2)** Confirm your personal safety, then immediately change ALL of your passwords. Even the ones you don't think they knew about or had access to. In the event of shared accounts, whoever reaches this stage first wins.

**3)** Delete histories for accounts when appropriate. Your watch history can be manipulated to include revolting and questionably legal content. Government watch lists should be avoided at all costs.

**4)** When updating your status on social media, make it seem like this was a peaceful, mutual parting of ways. The next person you date is likely to see this post at some point, so try to put a good light on it. You can tell them the truth privately, when the time is right.

**5)** For a period of time that equals the months or years you shared with your now ex, avoid all the places you used to frequent together. This will ensure that they cannot:
a) exact a devious revenge plot against you.
b) attempt to persuade you to take them back.
c) flaunt some super hot rebound lover in your face.

**6)** At this point, the only thing left to do is sit back and enjoy the fact that you just made the best—or possibly worst—decision of your life!

# POCKET-SIZED REFLECTIONS

Wounded, he buried his heart.
Fortunately, she carries a shovel.

This cage was
of my own making.
So too shall be
my wings.

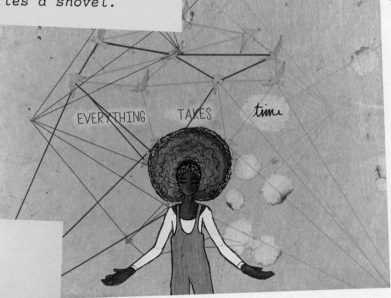

EVERYTHING TAKES time

The doctor called it
**cardiac dementia,**
'cause my love for you is
in **absentia.**

It was hard to leave,
but it was harder finding a reason to stay.

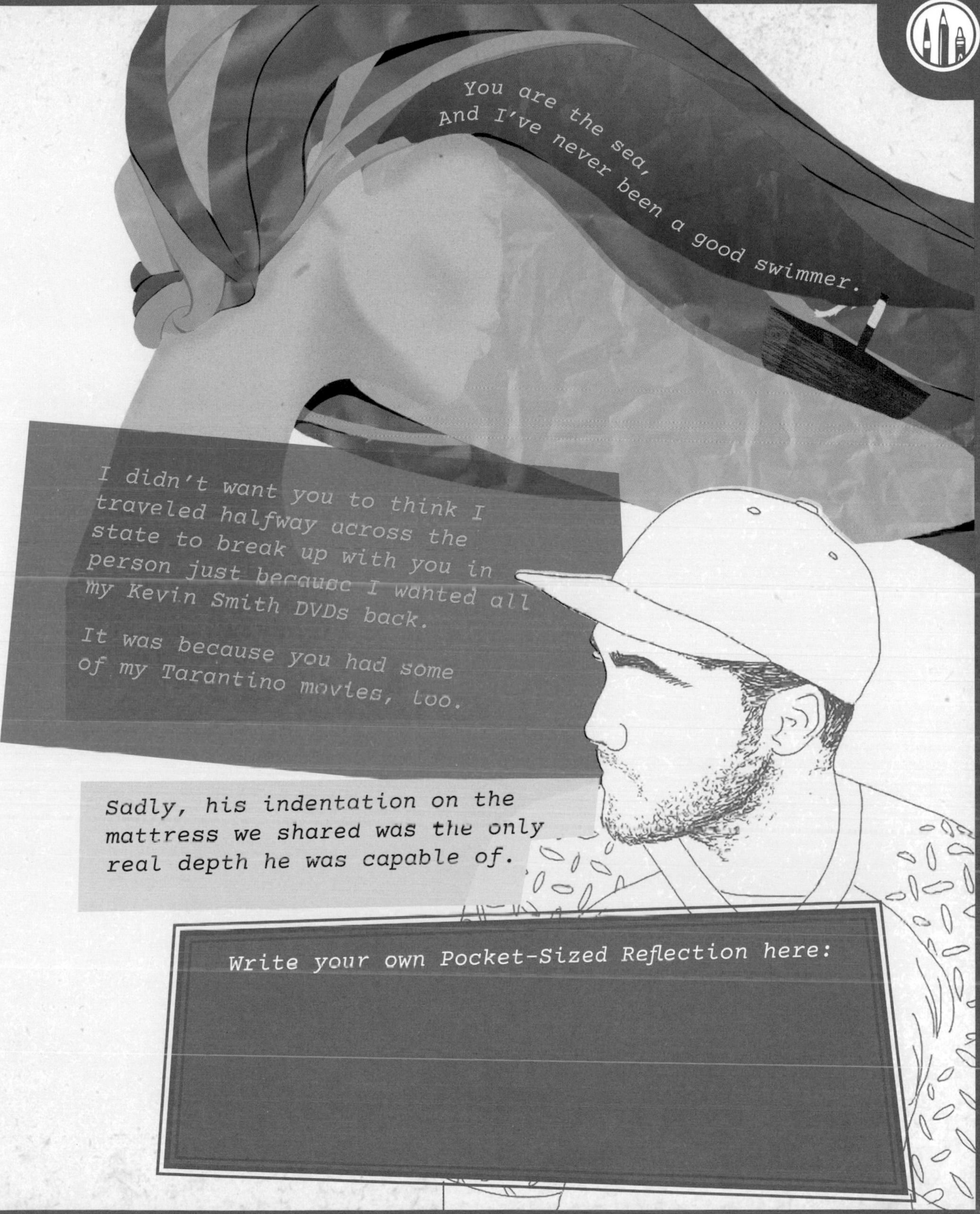

You are the sea,
And I've never been a good swimmer.

I didn't want you to think I
traveled halfway across the
state to break up with you in
person just because I wanted all
my Kevin Smith DVDs back.

It was because you had some
of my Tarantino movies, too.

Sadly, his indentation on the
mattress we shared was the only
real depth he was capable of.

Write your own Pocket-Sized Reflection here:

# WORD SEARCH

Peace and Quiet
Ready to Mingle
My Prerogative
Elbow Room
Independence
Free Rein

Party Time
Lone Wolf
Option
Fly
Single

Choice
Sweats
Solo
One
Self
Solitude

# WRITE YOUR OWN LOVE STORY

Once upon a time, I fell in love with a _____ person. They were everything I ever
                                        (adjective)

dreamed about. Not only were they _____, but they were also _____ and _____.
                                    (adjective)                    (adjective)      (adjective)

I would spend my time doodling their name in my _____ and daydreaming about
                                                  (object)

their _____. We slowly got to know each other while bonding over _____. Our
       (quality)                                                        (noun)

days were spent lying on the _____ and talking about _____.
                              (place)                       (object)

Things began to change when we reached _____. When we used to _____,
                                         (milestone)                  (verb)

now we would _____. Instead of telling me that they loved me, they started telling
              (verb)

me that they _____ me. I noticed them checking out the local _____. That was
              (verb)                                              (noun)

the final straw. I blew up right in the middle of the _____. I didn't even care that
                                                       (noun)

_____ saw me. I started yelling about their _____, and the way they _____.
 (noun)                                            (noun)                        (verb)

I capped it all off by throwing my _____ at them. When they didn't even _____,
                                    (object)                                   (verb)

I knew it was over for good. I stormed off to the _____, expecting them to follow.
                                                   (noun)

They didn't. Over the next few _____, I holed up and ate all the _____ while watching
                                (unit of time)                         (food)

_____. Even the song _____ couldn't cheer me up. I finally sat down and
 (movie)                   (song title)

wrote down every single _____ about them. All the times they _____. When they
                         (adjective)                               (verb)

told me you _____ me. I realized how much better off I was without them. I'm so glad I
             (verb)

came to my senses and kicked their _____ to the _____. Good riddance!
                                    (body part)        (noun)

# TINY BOYFRIENDS
## A SHORT STORY

In a moment of inspiration, Emilio broke from an argument with his boyfriend, Victor, and walked out the door. Days later, Victor called him. "So are you going to pick up your stuff from my house?" Victor asked.

Emilio arrived with a shoe box, but Victor had already assembled one for him. "It's not all here," Emilio said as he began raiding the home—turning out drawers and flipping over boxes. To Emilio's surprise, he discovered a tiny little man cowering under a pile of video games. It was a tiny version of his Victor. Emilio nabbed him and walked out the house with the rest of his things.

Emilio housed Tiny Victor in an empty pill bottle. Whenever melancholy struck, Emilio would crack it open. "The heart's feeling a bit sad today, little man. Join me for dinner?"

Tiny Victor was a far better listener than he recalled big Victor being. Of course, Tiny Victor could not talk, but this did not prevent a kinship between them. One day Tiny Victor swaggered over and raised Emilio's Q-Tips over his head like a circus strong man. This display of strength amused Emilio, and it became a routine in the house. Emilio would say, "How about this gargantuan baby carrot?" and Tiny Victor would tremble hoisting it over his head as Emilio applauded.

Emilio started taking him everywhere, but Emilio's companionship with Tiny Victor eventually began producing a yearning for big Victor. Tiny Victor would do his best to resolve this heartache. He'd lift toothpicks, chopsticks, pencils—whatever he could find—but none of it brought Emilio relief. Emilio began leaving him in the pill bottle for longer hours. Then, one day, Emilio forgot him at the office.

The next morning, Emilio arrived early and apologized profusely. Tiny Victor only gestured to be released from the bottle. Emilio did and continued with the speech that he'd been rehearsing all night.

"You're not Victor, but sometimes I like to believe you are," he said. "But the two of you are nothing alike. I can't decide if you are something of my doing or something of his. Do you know?"

Tiny Victor shook his head. He was stretching his legs over a pink eraser. "I think it's better if you stay in the car today," Emilio said. Tiny Victor glared at him and then took a paperclip and unbent it. Emilio shook his head and plopped Tiny Victor back into his bottle.

It was cold and raining outside, and Emilio paused to reconsider, but then felt confident that he could create a warm environment for Tiny Victor with a few tissues. Emilio placed Tiny Victor on the car's front seat and went to work building a nest. Just as it was nearing completion, Emilio caught sight of Tiny Victor rolling his bottle to the edge of the seat. Tiny Victor tumbled off the seat and out of the car.

Emilio scrambled to recover it, but the bottle was being carried away by a stream of rainwater that was running toward a large gutter. Tiny Victor lay relaxed in the orange container as he floated along the narrow conduit of water. Tiny Victor waved at Emilio. Emilio blew him a kiss. Tiny Victor beamed, flexed his tiny muscles, and then vanished down the sewer.

Suddenly, a pair of headlights flashed—temporarily blinding Emilio. He stood still, blinking to recover his vision. The car pulled alongside him, and the driver rolled down the passenger window.

"You're soaked," the man said as he opened the passenger-side door. Emilio stood in the rain trying to decide what to do next. He decided to step inside.

5

# DEPRESSION

Turns out single life is not all it's cracked up to be. The nights are getting cold and doubt is creeping in. Have you made a terrible, terrible mistake?

**This is the DEPRESSION chapter**—or the art of realizing hot one night stands won't keep you warm forever.

I'm sinking, slowly
Like quicksand I cannot move
Can't see a way out

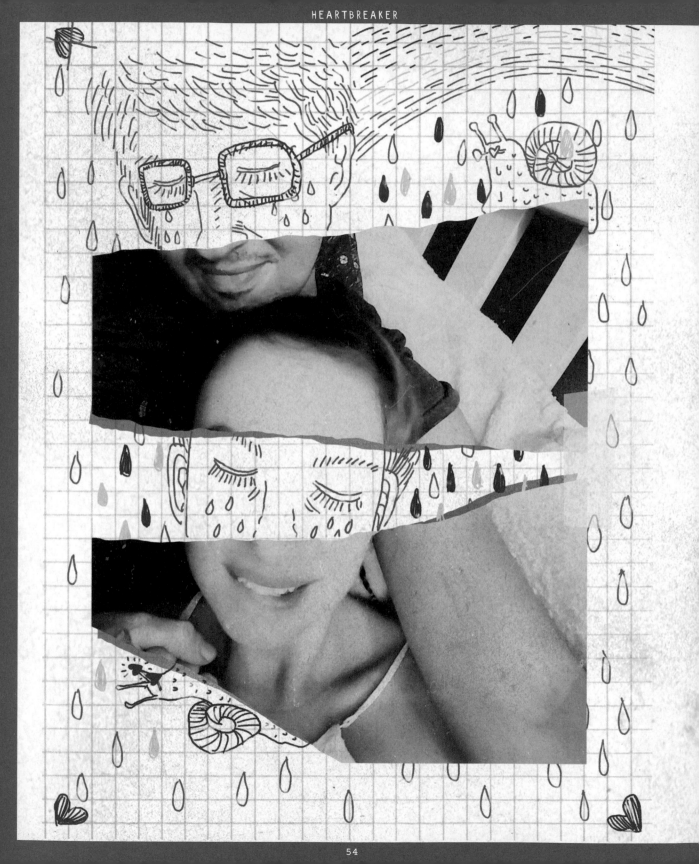

# WHAT DO YOU SEE?

my ex's smug face when our friends chose sides; they didn't choose mine

my ex trying to tell me I was making a mistake

my ex when they realized I meant every word

my ex when they said they loved me, before I mentioned splitting up

WRITE IT HERE...

my ex screaming at me that they never wanted to see me again and because of me they missed out on a huge promotion

my ex when I asked for visitation rights with the dog—they said no

my ex when they destroyed my Bowie albums and I said I hated them and never wanted them in my life ever again

# SELF-HELP BOOKSHELF

# LET THE OCEAN
## CARRY YOUR BURDENS...

Write a message in a bottle that only
the fishes will read...

# DEPRESSION CROSSWORD

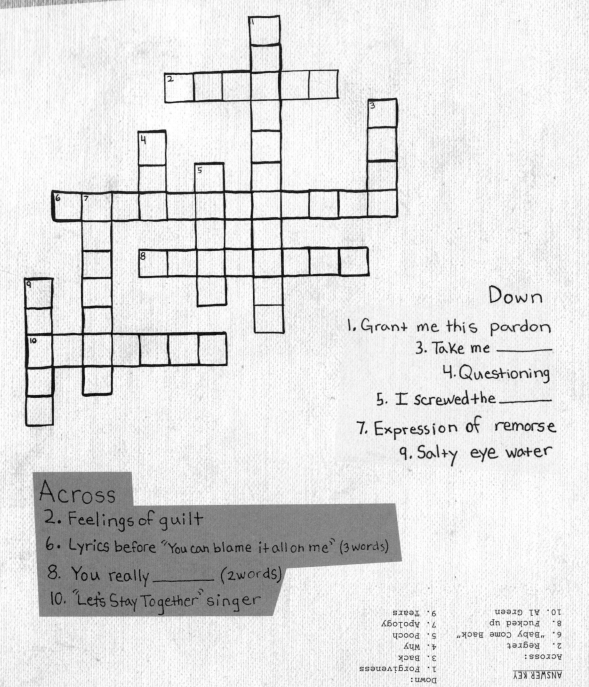

## Down

1. Grant me this pardon
3. Take me _____
4. Questioning
5. I screwed the _____
7. Expression of remorse
9. Salty eye water

## Across

2. Feelings of guilt
6. Lyrics before "You can blame it all on me" (3 words)
8. You really _____ (2 words)
10. "Let's Stay Together" singer

No cuddling in bed
Lonely ending of birthday
Broke it off too soon

Well, I've found someone new.
Someone who *actually* listens to me.
His name is Dr. Schwartz, and
he charges by the hour.

I let you go
long ago.
But somehow my heart
has yet to get
that memo.

too high the mountain
too low the sea
too blue the sky
too sad the me

too long the lonely
too many the tears
too short the love
too sad the years

too cold the heart
too much the pain
too gone the you
too late the rain

# 6
# BARGAINING

Everyone makes mistakes, and you've realized you made a big one. You want to give things another try but, for some reason, they won't return your calls.

**This is the BARGAINING chapter**—or the art of rebuilding bridges that you burned down yourself.

63

# HOW TO KEEP YOUR FRIENDS AFTER A BREAKUP

Okay, so you don't ever want to see your ex again, but your mutual friends are worth fighting for (most of them anyway). All's fair in post-love and war.

## BRIBE THEM

☐ Invite them to be your plus one, free of charge. All inclusive. First class. Complimentary champagne and chocolate box in the room. Airport transfer not included.

☐ Sign up for Netflix, Amazon Prime, and Hulu, and share your password with them. Be sure to remind them that you take internet security very seriously and change your passwords every thirty days.

## EMOTIONALLY BLACKMAIL THEM

☐ Explain how drained the whole experience has left you, and how you don't think you could cope with even one more thing going wrong, like your friendship.... (Cry.)

☐ Let them know if they side with your ex over you, you will make them pay (cry as you're saying it to them and then stop suddenly and stare at them until they're forced to swear loyalty to you). If necessary, make them pledge it over blood.

## LIE TO THEM

☐ Tell them how your ex used to tirelessly talk shit about them. Examples are always helpful, the pettier and bitchier, the better. If necessary, produce "evidence" such as text messages to back up your case (people with Photoshop skills and a penchant for cyber trashing are easy to befriend on the internet and have lots of spare time on their hands).

☐ Tell them you didn't start dating your new partner until after you had broken up with your ex. Be sure not to smirk.

I'M A PRICK, OBVIOUSLY.

BUT I'M YOUR PRICK, SO PLEASE FORGIVE ME.

# FRIENDS AND LOVERS
## THE SCIENTIFIC DIFFERENCES

### INTERACTIONS:

**FRIENDS**          **LOVERS**

SPORTS

FORGIVENESS          DINNER          BREAKFAST

HONESTY              MOVIES          DAYTIME TV

BRUNCH               LOVE            INTIMACY

                                     SEX

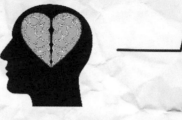

### KEY EQUATIONS:

FRIENDS + SEX = FRIENDS WITH BENEFITS

LOVERS + HONESTY = LOVERS WITH BENEFITS

NUMBER OF FRIENDS < NUMBER OF LOVERS = EXHAUSTION

### STATE CHANGES:

FRIENDS →→ APPLY HEAT AND FRICTION →→ LOVERS

**WARNING:** CONTRARY TO POPULAR BELIEF, PROCESS HAS BEEN PROVEN IRREVERSIBLE.

## CARDS TO WIN BACK YOUR EX →

Feeling like you made a mistake leaving your ex? No better way to express your regret than a card written by someone else.

# COUPONS TO WIN THEM BACK

So you screwed up. Admit it and promise not to take your ex for granted in the future.

As a sign of good faith, bestow upon them coupons that can be redeemed at any time. No ifs, ands, or buts from you.

ARGUMENTS LOYALTY CARD

SILENCE
SILENCE
SILENCE
SILENCE
SILENCE

7 SILENCES + 1 AUTO WIN

FREE
HEAD MASSAGE

FREE
BACK MASSAGE

FREE
EXOTIC MASSAGE

FREE
FOOT MASSAGE

## GET OUT OF JAIL FREE CARD

I'll visit your mom alone and make excuses for you so you can go out and drink with your friends.

## ACTIVITY OF YOUR CHOICE

(and I mean **anything**)

## OOH LA LA

Choose any roleplay you desire, and I'll get my own outfit to make your dreams come true —even if the polyester makes my skin break out.

## FREE RETURN

of our relationship!

## TRUTH OR DARE

Surprise! I'll finally go for dare this time. Dare me to ask if my best friend is up for that threesome you fantasized about.

## NO HOUSEHOLD CHORES

for the next two weeks if you just promise to stay in one night this week and watch a movie with me. You can even pick the movie!

## GET 1, GET ANOTHER FREE TESTICLE RUB!

Get those sex cravings out of the way and redeem this for a

## ONE-NIGHT FREEBIE

with no strings attached.

Redeem this and I'll finally try that

## ONE FREAKY THING

you talked about that I immediately shut down and never brought up again!

# 7

# ANGER

You decided to give them another chance. You kindly offered to get back together, but now THEY don't want to take YOU back! Who the hell do they think they are?

**This is the ANGER chapter**—or the art of reminding EVERYONE who broke up with whom in the first place.

If you were
so crushed
When I said
I was leaving,
Why have you
moved on?!

**THE NOT-SO-HIDDEN MESSAGE MIXTAPE**

1) Archive — *Fuck You*

2) Lily Allen — *Fuck You*

3) Anna David — *Fuck You*

4) Bad Religion — *Fuck You*

5) The Stiffs — *Fuck You*

6) Wesley Willis — *Fuck You*

7) CeeLo Green — *Fuck You*

You warrant no tears
But a thousand paper cuts
Should suffice nicely

# FINDING YOURSELF PERMANENTLY MARKED BY THE MEMORY OF YOUR EX? USE THIS GUIDE TO TURN THAT MARK INTO SOMETHING BRAND NEW!

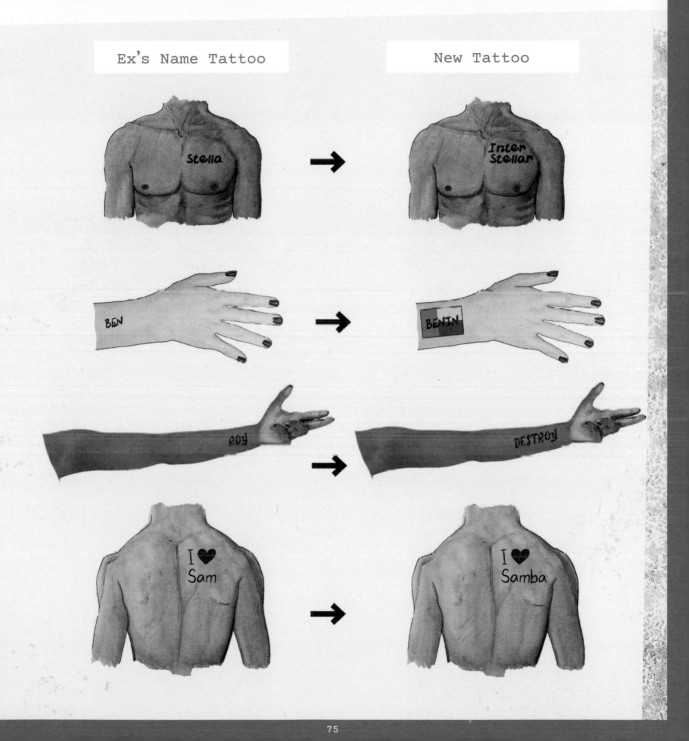

# OATMEAL RAISIN RAGE COOKIES

*With a Splash of the Cheapest Well Vodka You Can Find*

*Ingredients:
Raisins
Other Baking Shit
Oil
Pipette
The Cheapest Handle of
Well Vodka You Can Find

Instructions:

1. To begin, take one large swig of cheap-ass vodka straight from the plastic bottle.

2. To ensure cookies are infused with the suitable amount of anger, repeat step 1 until belligerence sets in.

3. Poorly impersonate your ex's dumb voice while slowly crushing individual raisins between your fingers. Imagine they are his shriveled testicles, if that helps.

4. Mix that other baking shit into a big bowl. Whatever. Who cares? Not you.

5. Add a splash of the poorly disguised rubbing alcohol you're swilling. And then take another large swig for yourself. One for the cookies, and one for you. That seems fair.

6. Accidentally spill the oil onto the floor. Make a half-assed attempt to scoop it up with your fingers and then give up, because he couldn't tell you how to live your life and neither will a stupid recipe book.

7. Combine the ingredients by pounding on them with that meat tenderizer that you never use because your ex was vegan. Batter that batter into submission.

9. ~~Smack~~ Slap the cookies on a baking pan and throw them into the oven. Turn the temperature all the way up, high as it'll go. Burn, cookies, burn! Burn them like you burned all his stupid clothes and photographs.

10. Have a nap. You've earned it.

11. Open or smash a window as your kitchen fills with thick black smoke billowing from the oven.

12. Remove the burned, charred remains of your cookies and sob uncontrollably as it occurs to you that you're staring at a metaphor for your relationship. Which is over, remember?

13. Soak up your tears with a sponge or rag. Wring them into a shot glass and place in the fridge.

8. Roll the disgusting mush into balls, fuck the size suggestion. Size DOES matter, and these cookies are gonna be HUGE.

14. Pour the remaining vodka into a large pitcher or bucket. Use a pipette to add in your now chilled tears, to taste.

15. Curl up into a pathetic ball on the kitchen floor, hug your salty vodka container close, and rock gently back and forth, back and forth, back and forth..........

the end

# THE SHIT THAT MY EX LEFT BEHIND
## (THAT I ALREADY SET ON FIRE)
### A WORD SEARCH

| A | C | R | E | E | P | Y | D | O | L | L | Q | S |
|---|---|---|---|---|---|---|---|---|---|---|---|---|
| P | U | A | P | I | C | K | A | X | E | R | D | H |
| U | G | B | Z | D | D | P | W | F | S | G | I | E |
| K | L | M | Q | D | R | E | S | T | T | P | K | A |
| A | Y | O | S | N | U | T | O | O | A | I | S | R |
| S | G | O | T | O | N | F | N | O | R | C | H | T |
| H | U | R | U | B | K | I | S | T | W | T | A | A |
| E | I | N | F | E | E | S | C | H | A | U | P | N |
| L | T | E | F | A | N | H | R | B | R | R | P | K |
| L | A | K | E | R | S | J | E | R | S | E | Y | L |
| N | R | O | D | D | E | P | E | U | T | O | T | E |
| E | P | R | I | T | X | A | K | S | I | F | R | T |
| C | I | B | G | R | T | E | D | H | C | H | E | I |
| K | C | V | U | I | A | U | V | Y | K | I | E | H |
| L | K | B | A | M | P | W | D | L | E | S | S | A |
| A | D | A | N | M | E | A | D | Y | T | M | S | T |
| C | U | I | A | E | H | B | D | K | S | O | K | E |
| E | Z | Q | L | R | F | H | N | A | T | M | E | D |
| I | H | D | Z | D | S | Q | E | J | U | H | T | B |
| Q | B | A | N | D | O | S | B | K | B | S | C | E |
| D | R | E | A | D | L | O | C | K | C | R | H | W |

PUKA SHELL NECKLACE
IPAD
LAKERS JERSEY
PICTURE OF HIS MOM
STUFFED IGUANA

DAWSON'S CREEK DVD
DRUNKEN SEX TAPE
HAPPY TREES SKETCH
BROKEN ROOMBA
CREEPY DOLL

STAR WARS TICKET STUB
HEART ANKLET I HATED
UGLY GUITAR PICK
BEARD TRIMMER
TOOTHBRUSH

DREADLOCK
DILDO
PICKAXE
PET FISH

# COLORING PAGE

# MAYBE YOU CAN
## CONNECT THESE DOTS.

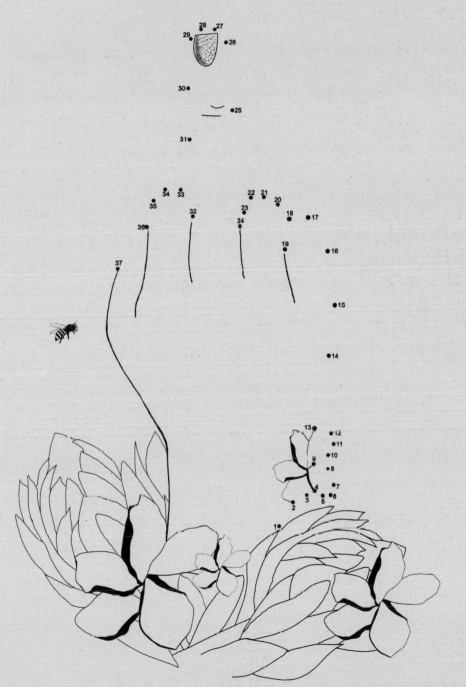

# 8
# DENIAL

Who? Oh, them? You haven't thought about them in ages. You're so thrilled that they've found happiness without you. You're doing great without them. Yeah, really really great...

**This is the DENIAL chapter**—or the art of convincing yourself you haven't made a horrible mistake.

# No, I'm not crying

No, I'm not crying
I'm coming down with the flu
My eyes are sensitive and I've been sweeping
It's the dust, it's not you

No, I'm not crying
I just poked myself in the eye
I've been laughing for a while
And this is my face when I'm high

No, I'm not crying
I'm trying out new contact lenses
It's probably an allergic reaction
Damn, these candles must be scented

No, I'm not crying
I've been staring at the sun
Got new makeup, went out clubbing
I'm so happy that we're done

Doing great.
I'm not
Regretting it and
I'm completely
Sure
I wasn't
Too impulsive
I'm just
Looking to the future
Not
Living in the past
I'm
Happy again
Can't even imagine being
With you
I want to be
Single now.

Single now.
I want to be
With you
Can't even imagine being
Happy again
I'm
Living in the past
Not
Looking to the future
I'm just
Too impulsive
I wasn't
Sure
I'm completely
Regretting it and
I'm not
Doing great.

Dear Reader:

Welcome to the BROKEN-HEARTED side of the book. What you are about to read is an ode to a human experience that most everyone—man or woman, gay or straight, rich or poor, crazy or sane, Slytherin or Gryffindor—can relate to. Yes, friend. We are referring to getting dumped.

Whether it be a devastating end to a thirty-year relationship resulting in heartbreak or a swift blow to the ego following a calamitous Tinder date, we've all experienced heartbreak in one way or another.

Getting your heart broken may be universal, but the way that we react and cope with it is unique to every individual. And that, dear reader, is what this book is all about.

People all over the world contributed personal stories from their own experiences with heartbreak. Writers, illustrators, and graphic designers collaborated on the following pages to paint a diverse picture of the story of the BROKEN HEARTED.

If you've ever been broken up with, read this book. Hold it, hug it, weep onto its pages, love it like the child who could have been if you'd ended up with so and so, BURN it (if you're into that kind of thing...). Do whatever YOU like because this book is by you, for you, and about you. This is *The Art of Breaking Up*—the BROKEN-HEARTED side.

With Shattered Love,
Your Fellow Broken Hearteds

P.S. To those of you who haven't experienced the festering, unrelenting, and unforgiving ache of the ol' myocardium; to those who are always the ones doing "the dumping," we say, hey asshole—flip the book over and start from the other end because we simply *cannot* with you. Or stick around. It might do you some good to flip through the following pages and get a glimpse at the irrevocable damage you have caused.

# CONTENTS

Chapters outline the events leading up to a breakup and the psychological stages of healing that follow. Much like a catastrophic earthquake, breaking up isn't a singular event. There are the initial tremors that signal the inevitable, tragic destruction. Then, once all of the dust has settled, the rubble can be cleared and a stronger foundation can be built.

# 1

# EARLY WARNING SIGNS

They're not answering your texts. They're not making eye contact. They're spending an awful lot of time at the "gym." Are you growing apart, or are you just being paranoid?

**This is the EARLY WARNING SIGNS chapter**—or the art of secretly reading their text messages in the middle of the night.

You used to watch rom-coms with me.
Now you're just looking for action.

WARNING

KEEPS
SECRETS

## Last Year

We were all over each other.

Your lips were soft and your kisses took my breath away.

You forgot my birthday but bought me flowers to make up for it.

When I called you, we would stay on the phone for hours and talk about nothing at all.

We watched movies on the couch all tangled up in each other.

You carried me to the roof just to see the sunset reflected in my eyes.

You thought my snoring was cute.

You held my hand everywhere we went.

Friends combined our names and called us "Kiffany."

## This Year

We're all over the place.

Your kisses have a lingering aftertaste of death.

You forgot my birthday and scribbled "age is a construct" on a greasy napkin.

When I called you, a man picked up the phone and he seemed to be out of breath.

You read in the recliner, and I watch TV on the couch alone.

Your post of me and a camel with the same lazy eye went viral.

You suggested we sleep in separate rooms.

You walk at least two steps ahead of me at all times.

Our friends call us "Turt."

WANDERING
EYE

Funny how quickly things can change. Write your own before and after list, noting how your signficant other treated you at the blissful beginning of your relationship and towards the bitter end.

The Blissful Beginning

The Bitter End

This specialized quiz will help you find out if you're really just being a "paranoid freak" or if you should take the warning signs a little more seriously to avoid getting caught off guard.

For each question, choose the answer that most accurately applies to your current situation.

Good luck!

# ARE YOU ABOUT TO GET DUMPED?

## 1 - You're approaching taking this test with:

a. A cocky smile on your face and plans to go on a date night.
b. A nervous little laugh and a glance over your shoulder to make sure nobody's watching.
c. A sinking feeling in your stomach, shaking hands, and a bottle of tequila.

## 2 - The last time you had sex:

a. You had amazing chemistry and eye contact with your partner.
b. You did orgasm but only because you "helped yourself out."
c. Your partner was looking at someone else's picture on their phone the whole time.

## 3 - When you tell your partner you love them, they:

a. Tell you they love you more.
b. Reply with "ditto" if they can't pretend they didn't hear it.
c. Go off about how you're pressuring them to "verbalize such a complex emotion in very simplistic terms."

## 4 - When you unexpectedly touch your partner in public, they:

a. Cuddle into it.
b. Take it for a few seconds and then pretend to need to use the bathroom.
c. Jump as if a stranger had just groped them on the subway and roll their eyes at you in reprimand.

## 5 - When you wake up feeling sick, your partner:

a. Can't do enough to make sure you're comfortable and cared for.
b. Sends a couple of texts throughout the day to check if it's something contagious.
c. Immediately takes a shower and doesn't touch you for the following three to five days.

**6 – On your last birthday, your partner:**

a. Created a countdown calendar for the big day and showered you with presents all month long.
b. Sang "Happy Birthday" and gave you a gift card they'd received on Christmas.
c. Forgot the date until three days later, when you made the information public on social media.

**7 – The last time your partner went on a business trip, you:**

a. Skyped every day, despite the time difference.
b. Felt a little too happy to have the bed all to yourself and some days "forgot" to call.
c. Automatically assumed they were going to cheat on you and weren't even that upset about it.

**8 – When you plan a surprise for your partner, they:**

a. Get so excited they look like a little kid at Disneyland.
b. Humor you but are clearly expecting to be embarrassed at some point.
c. Start an epic argument that causes you to miss the surprise.

**9 – You've just told the same joke you tell at every party.**

   **Your partner:**

a. Laughs like it's their first time hearing it.
b. Cracks a forced smile just before taking a sip of their wine.
c. Fails to hide an obvious eye roll as they mutter a "Jesus" under their breath.

**10 – It's your turn to pick a movie. Your partner:**

a. Tells you how much they wanted to see that movie.
b. Is fine about it as long as they can sleep through it.
c. Guilts you into watching what they want and then blames you when they realize what a bad choice it was.

**Your Results:**

**Mostly As:** Congratulations! You've found yourself a good one. They're not going anywhere, and—if we were you—we'd start planning our wedding.

**Mostly Bs:** Relationships need work, and you need to do something fast if you want to keep yours intact. We advise anything short of having a baby.

**Mostly Cs:** We're sorry friend, but the breakup is coming. You know it, they know it, and our advice is for you to be the one doing the breaking up. At least you can save face.

My hand was always clammy.
That's not why you stopped holding it.

KINDLY *respond* BY THE SIXTEENTH OF MARCH

CAN ATTEND ☐   CAN NOT ATTEND ☐

NOTE Sorry! I'll come to your next one!

PALOMINO BLACKWING·PEARL

You see
my cousin's
save-the-date
card for six
months out.

You go as white
as the paper.

Guess my RSVP
doesn't include
a plus one.

He said he doesn't
believe in monogamy.

He doesn't know
my middle name.

He asked for my best
friend's number.

# CONNECTING THE DOTS...

# POCKET-SIZED REFLECTIONS

You were so disappointed when the doctor called with my results...he said the tumor was benign.

I was the punch line of all your bad jokes.

We were always amazing in bed,

but we never did get that coffee.

## 2
# THE LAST GASP

It's the fourth quarter of your relationship and there's less than a minute left on the clock. Time for the ultimate Hail Mary play.

**This is the LAST GASP chapter**—or the art of the grand, but ultimately futile, romantic gesture.

My man says
we might need a break.

But I know
that'd be a mistake.

So I'll make him stay
the one foolproof way:

With daily mounds of pancakes!

# THE ORIGAMI GUIDE TO THE LAST GASP

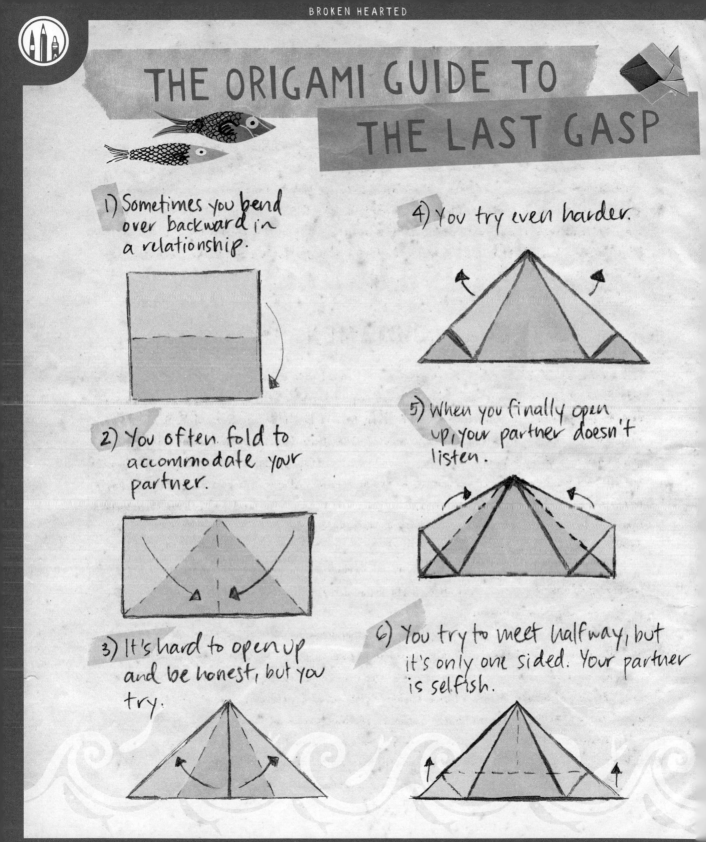

1) Sometimes you bend over backward in a relationship.

2) You often fold to accommodate your partner.

3) It's hard to open up and be honest, but you try.

4) You try even harder.

5) When you finally open up, your partner doesn't listen.

6) You try to meet halfway, but it's only one sided. Your partner is selfish.

7) To stay afloat, your partner finally folds. It's too late.

8) As time goes by, you realize you're in a sinking ship. You... capsize.

10) You've reached the end, but it's okay. There are other fish in the sea.

9) It feels like you're drowning. You need to separate and break things up.

# THE LAST SUPPER
## A SHORT STORY

I've been at the supermarket for what seems like hours. I have scanned and googled the nutritional information on every single product just for a meal for my wife, Caz. Protein, carbs, fat content. I mean, I know she has taken this health kick seriously, so I should too. If I am going to make this marriage work I have to make the effort to get it back on track.

Mom picked up the kids to have them overnight. At home, I turn on some sexy music and write the menu. I smell like someone else with the aftershave she bought me, but she likes it, so I'm wearing it. I text Caz to say I have something special planned when she gets back from work. She's always loved romantic surprises. Well, she used to.

No answer.

A few hours later, Caz comes home from work and says she got the text but forgot to text back. She says she has a gym session booked with Adam. Could we do the whole "meal thing" tomorrow? I should have known, apparently I never listen to her. There is nothing to listen to because she barely looks up from her phone. My whole inner being is deflated. "Sure, whatever you want," I say.

I don't want to cause another argument where she says I'm being inconsiderate of "her time." I just automatically try to keep the peace now. Caz wants to focus on her health and happiness by going to the gym and taking control of herself again. Adam, her personal trainer, has been working with her, helping her achieve her goals, even if her goals cost $85 an hour. I don't have a problem paying for it if it helps her feel better about herself. Even if that means I never eat another carb in front of her again.

Before Caz leaves for the gym, she glances at the table and gives me a small smile. Neither of us say anything. I'm left with the sexy music, weird aftershave, a dinner for two, and an empty seat that reflects how I feel. It's hopeless. Dinner for two? Who was I kidding? There have been three people in this marriage for the last few months, and like a fool, I've been pretending everything is okay. You can't save a relationship when there's only one of you in it.

I look at the pathetic meal in front of me and suddenly I'm not hungry anymore. I pick up the menu and decide to rewrite it.

## STARTER

Heart-shaped salmon mousse terrine made with non-dairy cream that I had to whip at full speed for at least two hours because it has no fat in it to actually make a mousse. I did consider just getting normal cream and lying to you, but I know that you would be devastated at such a betrayal. It would appear, however, that lying about betrayal isn't a problem for you.

## MAIN COURSE

Grilled chicken with extra protein and a side of extra protein and lots of green, tasteless vegetables because I can't sauté them in garlic and butter or drown them in meat sauce. I have washed away any trace of carbs from the menu. In fact, I have banished them from the house. All those tasty, filling, and complex carbs that cause you to freak out, in case you actually want to have that feeling of fullness for an iota of a second are all gone. I know Adam wouldn't approve. We wouldn't want to upset him, would we?

## DESSERT

Sparkling water with a slice of lime and a sprig of mint. Don't worry, I have checked. The bubbles have no fat in them. I'll have the gin, because we wouldn't want the trace sugar in it to turn into complex carbs and upset Adam.

Instead of wine with the meal, I have chosen a charcoal and wheatgrass combo that looks like something I would clean the bottom of a boat with.

I put the pen down. I don't feel any better. It's over, isn't it?

# RELATIONSHIP OUIJA BOARD

SUMMON THE SPIRIT OF YOUR RECENTLY DECEASED
RELATIONSHIP AND ASK THE QUESTIONS THAT YOU
NEVER COULD BEFORE THE BREAKUP, LIKE...

Are there any spirits of my
previous relationship here with me
right now? Good or evil?

Come forward and speak with me.

I miss you.

How are you doing?
Why did you leave me?
Do you ever think of me?
Are you angry with me?
Did you ever really love me?
What's your fondest memory of us?
Can we still be friends?

Before I forget, what is the Wi-Fi
password you set for my apartment?

Okay, bye for now.

Feel free to come back and haunt me.

# CLINGY COUPONS

Whatever it is, I'm sorry. I'll make it up to you!
Here, have some coupons! Redeemable with me only! xoxo

# COLORING PAGE

WHEN YOU KNOW THE "TALK" IS COMING, BUT YOU WANT TO PLAY YOUR LAST CARD—HERE ARE SOME GREAT ARGUMENTS TO GUILT YOUR PARTNER INTO NOT BREAKING UP WITH YOU:

You can't leave me now...

I just got a heart transplant so I could *literally* give you mine, and I even had them put it in a fancy jar!

You can't leave me now...

I already have the swing, the goat, and the sexy guy from the other night at the club, waiting at the house to help us fulfill your every sexual fantasy! All the forms are signed too.

You can't leave me now...

I've just finished our matching sweaters made from the hair I've been collecting from your brush and shower drain since we started dating!

You can't leave me now...

I just booked your favorite band to play at your surprise birthday party that I'm throwing for two-hundred of your closest friends and family!

You can't leave me now...

I just baked a seventeen-tiered chocolate cake made with cocoa beans that I personally picked in Brazil to celebrate our seventeen days together!

You can't leave me now...

I just bought nonrefundable deluxe tickets for a three-month transatlantic newlywed's cruise!

You can't leave me now...

I just got a tattoo of Mount Rushmore on my back with different versions of your face instead of the presidents!

# 3
# THE BREAKUP

Brace yourself. It doesn't matter whether you know it's coming or if it comes completely out of the blue, this isn't going to be fun.

**This is the BREAKUP chapter**—or the art of not crying in public.

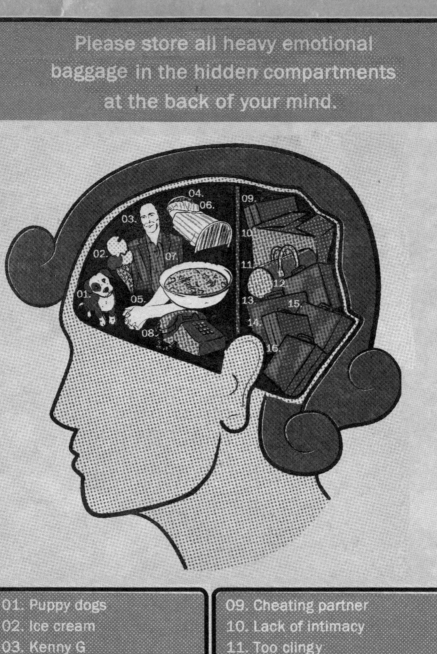

Please store all heavy emotional baggage in the hidden compartments at the back of your mind.

01. Puppy dogs
02. Ice cream
03. Kenny G
04. Clean sheets
05. Holding hands in silence
06. Lazy Sundays
07. Chicken soup
08. Calling in sick

09. Cheating partner
10. Lack of intimacy
11. Too clingy
12. Jealousy
13. Bullied at school
14. Co-worker ate my sandwich
15. Pulled my back doing that
16. Father issues

Did someone break your heart?
Return the favor by making a

# HEART PIÑATA

## What to do

1. Mix flour, water, and salt. Stir the mess you made until it thickens.

2. Tear the bad news into strips that are approx. 1 inch wide and 6 inches long.

3. Inflate the balloon. Tape some crumbled newspaper on it to form a heart shape.

4. Dip the paper strips in your mess and apply them crisscross to the heart in three layers. But leave the balloon knot exposed!

5. When dry, paint it bloodred and let dry again. Have a break to cry! You deserve it.

6. Make a small incision below the knot to deflate from your time together, seal it, and string it.

### Now, grab a baseball bat and BREAK THAT FUCKING HEART!

## What you need

2 cups of water
2 cups of flour
1 tbsp. of salt
1 balloon
Some newspaper (with bad news)
Some red paint (close to blood)

Also requires
**memorabilia
as filling!**

# HOW TO DEAL WITH A BREAKUP
## A DECISION TREE

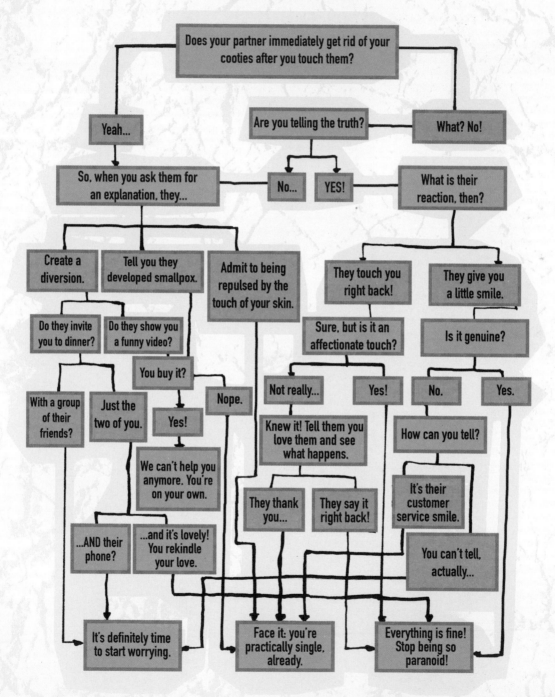

# The Post-Breakup Relationship Survey

*Please, do not crumple, rip, and/or burn this survey before
you read it through. Thank you for your understanding.*

Dear Breakup Recipient,

It seems I've just broken up with you, and I'm sorry for any inconvenience
the aforementioned process may have caused you.

However, even though I'm no longer committed to you, I am committed to
providing as positive a breakup experience as possible for all my future
failed lovers henceforward.

So, with your honest feedback on this short survey, I expect to be able to
perfect the breakup process within the next seven to eight months.

Best regards,

Your ex

. . . . . . . . . . . . . . . . . . . . . . . . . . . . . . . . . . . . . . . . . . . . . . . . . . . . . . . . . . . . . . . . . . . . . . . . . .

*For this next section of the survey, please mark your answers
with a check instead of a cross to keep the negativity out.*

**For statistical purposes, check the
reason I gave you for the breakup:**

( ) We've grown apart.

( ) I met someone else.

( ) It's not you, it's me.

**How do you feel right now?
(check all that apply)**

( ) Relieved.          ( ) Surprised.

( ) Confused.          ( ) Devastated.

( ) Pretty pissed.     ( ) Other: _____

**How would you rate my choice of location?**

( ) Actually, quite lovely.          ( ) Fine, I guess?

( ) Like I was paying attention     ( ) You can go screw yourself!
   to that, you asshat.

( ) Just terrible.

*Next Page* ⟶

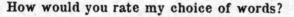

**How would you rate my choice of words?**

( ) So articulate I almost apologized myself.

( ) It was fine.  ( ) Meh.

( ) Could've been worse.  ( ) Horrible.

( ) Piss off, will ya?

**What was your favorite part of the breakup?**

( ) My strong empathy.

( ) The refreshments I provided.

( ) The data and detailed graphs that I provided.

**How could I improve the breakup experience in the future?**

( ) By bringing tissues.

( ) By not breaking up.

( ) By never dating anyone ever again.

( ) By offering breakup sex and/or other goods.

**What was your least favorite part of the breakup?**

( ) The timing.

( ) The devastating realization that it's over.

( ) The feedback survey.

**Would you recommend me to a friend or family member?**

( ) Yes  Name: _____  Phone Number: _____

( ) No!

( ) You're a sick person.

........................................................................................................................

*Thank you for taking the time to complete this survey! At the end of the year, all completed surveys will be entered into a drawing where the winner will receive one chance to win me back (non-exchangeable).*

# THE BREAKUP LETTER

Your now-ex has delivered you a formal letter of resignation from your relationship. So much for a two week's notice.

This letter appears two more times throughout this side of the book, but each time with a very different perspective. (there's nothing a little pen can't fix.)

[Broken Hearted],

I'll get straight to the point:

I want to break up.

You probably don't know all the reasons why I want to - or maybe you do. Honestly, all I used to think is I wouldn't know how I'd live without you. But as it turns out, I need to live without you. The fights, the resentment, and the time spent growing apart... This was never going to work with you. We have too much holding us down, and nothing in common. And... I don't know if I love you anymore. There's nothing that you, I, or we can do to bring us back. I thought I'd just save you the trouble and get it over with. There isn't anything we can do. We're just not meant to be together.

I'm breaking up with you.

I'm sorry.

[Heartbreaker]

# The Great Treatise of Strategies and Tactics in the Custody Battle for your Mutual Friends

### The Initiation of Disinformation

Spread lies; tell tall tales. Maybe your former significant other is a gossip and is revealing all of your friend's secrets. It doesn't matter if it is true, only that it is believed.

### The "This-Is-Awkward" Ambush

Your mutual friends and ex are out on the town, and you know their itinerary. Show up and encounter them when they least expect it. Make it as awkward as possible so that your friends feel bad and schedule a hangout with you for that week. Bonus points if you can schedule a brunch.

### The "I-Just-Can't-Deal" Feint, a.k.a. All-Out Guilt Attack

Have your friends know how hard this breakup has been on you, and if you lost your friends too you'd be a blubbering mess for the rest of your life. Tears are your ammunition. Use them. Initiate the attack with a lot of heavy sighs and ho-hums until someone asks what's wrong.

### The Great Gift-Giving Gambit

People love stuff. They probably love stuff more than they love you. So give them stuff, and they will love you, the giver of stuff. Invite them to lavish dinners, shopping sprees at the mall, and the coup de grâce is a brand-new puppy or kitten, with a name similar to your name to always remind them of you, the giver of stuff.

> **WARNING**: Following any of the above advice may backfire and blow up in your face, leaving you with no friends at all. Caution in employing any of the strategies.

# WHO WOULD ILLUSTRATE YOUR BREAKUP?

I give an ultimatum.

She leaves me and our daughter for a man our mutual ex-friend introduced to her at a club. They've known each other one week.

I cry. I flip a table. I drink and smoke and make an ass of myself. I punch a hole in the wall and cry some more. A foot fetishist on a dating site tells me I'm too vanilla.

Eventually, the tears run out. Time passes. Distance heals.

She joins us for Christmas. She says she and her new boyfriend have been fighting.

She asks if I ever wonder whether we should get back together.

I barely notice. I'm busy messaging a cute writer online, and she hasn't mentioned feet once.

# BREAKUP BINGO

| BOUGHT YOURSELF A CAT | THEY FOUND SOMEONE NEW | THEY BROKE YOUR HEART | DECIDED TO STAY FRIENDS | EATING YOUR FEELINGS |
|---|---|---|---|---|
| YOU BROKE THEIR HEART | LEFT THEIR STUFF ON THE LAWN | BURNED ALL YOUR PHOTOGRAPHS | BROKE UP VIA TEXT | THEY TOOK THE DOG |
| DRUNK DIALED YOUR EX | THEY DUMPED YOU | FREE SPACE | HAD POST-BREAKUP SEX | KEPT THEIR SWEET DVD COLLECTION |
| SWORE OFF DATING FOREVER | YOU GOT OVER THEM | BITCHING SESSION WITH FRIENDS | CHANGED THE LOCKS | THEY CHEATED |
| EXHAUSTING CRYING SESSION | THREE DAYS TOTALLY HAMMERED | THEY LIED TO YOU | YOU DUMPED THEM | YOU FOUND SOMEONE NEW |

# 4
# DENIAL

This can't be happening. You'd both had some wine. Maybe it was a joke? Maybe it was a dream? Of course it's not REALLY over. It can't be over. It's not over. Definitely not.

**This is the DENIAL chapter**—or the art of pretending nothing has changed.

The one you love now wants you gone?
Throw Rose-Tinted Glasses on!
SATISFACTION 100% GUARANTEED
100% guaranteed to make even the worst breakup seem like just a terrible misunderstanding.
Warning: Incompatible with common sense, dignity, self-worth, or moving on. Repeated use may result in actual heartbreak.
YES, IT'S REALLY OVER. STOP ASKING.
8

# BLIND FAITH!
## the game

BLIND FAITH!

It's over!

Reasonable Explanation

The Game For Those Who Speak The Truth ...

And For Those Who Don't Listen !

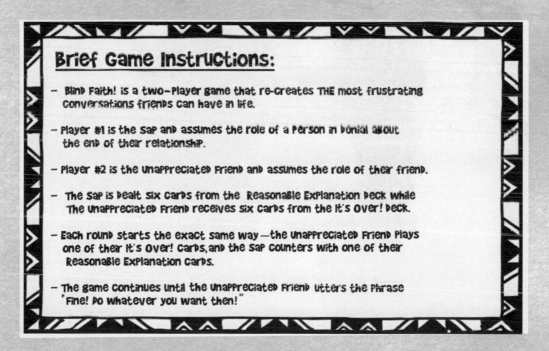

## Brief Game Instructions:

- Blind Faith! is a two-player game that re-creates THE most frustrating conversations friends can have in life.

- Player #1 is the sap and assumes the role of a person in denial about the end of their relationship.

- Player #2 is the unappreciated friend and assumes the role of their friend.

- The sap is dealt six cards from the Reasonable Explanation deck while the unappreciated friend receives six cards from the It's Over! deck.

- Each round starts the exact same way—the unappreciated friend plays one of their It's Over! cards, and the sap counters with one of their Reasonable Explanation cards.

- The game continues until the unappreciated friend utters the phrase "Fine! Do whatever you want then!"

## It's Over! cards

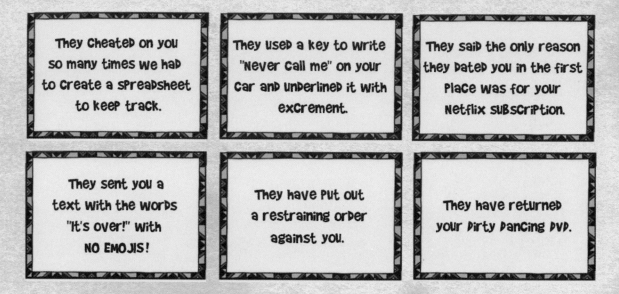

They cheated on you so many times we had to create a spreadsheet to keep track.

They used a key to write "Never call me" on your car and underlined it with excrement.

They said the only reason they dated you in the first place was for your Netflix subscription.

They sent you a text with the words "It's over!" with NO EMOJIS!

They have put out a restraining order against you.

They have returned your Dirty Dancing DVD.

## Reasonable Explanation cards

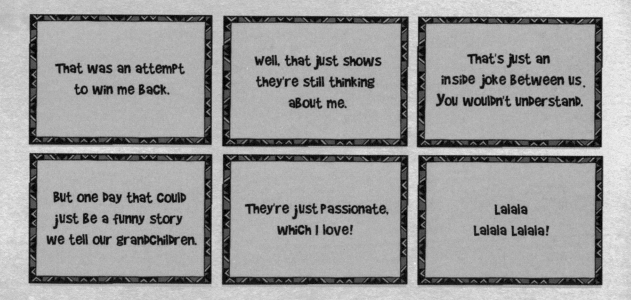

That was an attempt to win me back.

Well, that just shows they're still thinking about me.

That's just an inside joke between us. You wouldn't understand.

But one day that could just be a funny story we tell our grandchildren.

They're just passionate, which I love!

Lalala Lalala Lalala!

# DENIAL CITY

## POPULATION: YOU

While you're here, check out our main attractions. All perfectly suited to YOU, just like your ex was!

## The On-a-Break Hotel:

No minimum stay, because you won't be here long. Right? RIGHT?! You're just on a break. Leave any time or stay as long as you want! There's no long-term commitments, because you're getting back with your ex any day now.

## The Grand Library of Misinterpreted Text Messages:

This gem is a historic monument updated in the late 1900s and again in the early 2000s. Previously the Library of Misinterpreted Voicemails, and before that the Library of Misinterpreted Letters!!

But what did they really mean when they said that? The questions are all answered in this gorgeous hall of history. Reread paragraphs to one-word responses, over and over again... search for meaning all day long.

## The World-Famous Winemback Mall:

Need a new hairstyle? That fun, trendy outfit? Or a complete makeover?? This is a fan favorite in our town. People from all over the world shop 'til they DROP! No relationship is on the rocks because of personality (duh!)... It's always something that can be fixed with a little charge to the ol' plastic! So visit all of our shops, from Look21forever to S&M, Groomingdale's, and More!!

## Stalker-Central Café:

After creating the "New You" at the Winemback Mall, come over and enjoy our best coffee and pastries while checking your ex's social media over and over again, hoping for a post that might subtly be referring to you! Did you check out the song they shared recently? There might be something in the lyrics! Play it over the speakers and ask the other patrons. They might be able to help you out.

Make sure to visit our "sexy selfie" zone with free unlimited Wi-Fi. This way, you can upload all of your new pictures while looking fab and have your ex come crawling back to you!

## Grand Reflection Pool:

Take a stroll along the Grand Reflection Pool and reflect on every detail of your relationship. Think about what you could've done better or what you might still be able to do to get them back. The pool is only inches deep with no risk of drowning, intentional or accidental!

*"Images in pool may not reflect reality."*

# (RE)WRITE YOUR OWN HISTORY

They said they didn't love you anymore, but there was clearly A LOT more to the story. We've given you the first line—now it's up to you to write why they REALLY broke up with you.

Something wasn't quite right that morning...

# THE ~~BREAKUP~~ LOVE LETTER

[Broken Hearted],

~~I'll get straight to~~ The point~~—~~

I want to break ~~up~~

~~You probably don't know all the~~ ~~reasons why I want to~~ ~~but maybe you~~ ~~do. The things I've just realized which~~ is
I wouldn't know how I'd live without you. ~~But~~ As it turns out, I need ~~to~~ ~~live without you. The fights, the~~ ~~resentment, and the time spent~~ ~~growing apart. I think we're never~~ ~~going to work with~~ you. We have too much ~~holding us down~~ ~~and nothing~~ in common. And... ~~I don't know if~~ I love you. ~~anymore. There's nothing~~ ~~that you, I, or~~ we ~~we~~ can do ~~so I am~~ ~~as just as I thought I'd just save you~~ ~~the trouble, and get it over with.~~ ~~There isn't~~ anything ~~left to~~ ~~make just like move back~~ together.

I'm ~~breaking up~~ with you.

~~I'm sorry.~~

[Heartbreaker]

# THINGS YOU TELL YOUR FAMILY WHEN YOU'RE TOTALLY NOT IN DENIAL

- We filed the wrong form by mistake—Annuity/Annulment, what's the difference?

- She said she had to work on herself before she could be worthy of me. I agreed.

- He says he really loves me, but right now he just needs to put his focus on his true passion...reviewing sneakers on YouTube.

- He went on a fishing trip and called to say he found a "great catch," but it's been three weeks and honestly that fish had to have gone bad by now...

- She's just been really busy working on the pitch for a new show. It's called *The Real Housewives of America's Next Top Ninja Bachelor*. It's probably going to take a while, because she has to find all the best ninjas in America who are currently married, but like, maybe won't be for long, and then talk to their wives.

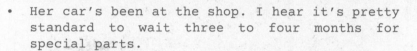

- Her car's been at the shop. I hear it's pretty standard to wait three to four months for special parts.

- She didn't mean to leave me at the altar. Her Uber took her to the wrong church. Some kind of GPS error. It's okay though. We'll reschedule.

- He moved out because of his allergies. Something in that apartment just didn't sit well with him.

- She asked me not to call after 7 p.m. Apparently that's when her brother visits, and they don't want to be disturbed playing backgammon.

- He only moved back to his mom's garage because she has enough room there for his DJ equipment.

- DMV clerk is a high-travel position.

- We're still together, but we go out separately. And we sleep in separate beds. With different people.

If I could
Unmake this mess
Would
I

me
without
you
is better than
me
with
you

you
with
me
is better than
you
without
me

I
Would
Unmake this mess
If I could

# Single Living

*Make the most of your single status.*
*Guest stylist Josie shares her home, favorite things, and tips.*

**INSIDE HOMES**
*Josie,*
*Recording Artist*

*HIS MIRRORS*
Leave them if you can't reach
to remove them.

*HIS SURFBOARD*
Keep it, as you might learn to
use it one day.

*STORAGE BOXES*
Keep his shirts neat, ordered,
and dust-free.

*COUPLES PORTRAITS*
Keep the ones where your hair still
looks amazing!

*SEX TOYS*
Keep them just in case he calls.

*BLACK BEDSHEETS*
Adds moody atmosphere, and
they were his favorite.

*HIS BOOKS*
Keep them! They make you
look smart.

*"HIS" PUPPY*
*Pending the custody court case.

**HOT TIP**

**SECRET ADMIRER FLOWERS**
Flowers brighten any room, and your family,
guests, and ex-boyfriends won't know you actually
bought them yourself.

29

# 5
# ANGER

That ungrateful, low life loser thinks they can do better than you!? Time to start planning your sweet, sweet revenge.

**This is the ANGER chapter**—or the art of making a bonfire out of their personal belongings.

RIGHT BACK AT YA!!

Adele - Hello
ABBA - Thank You for the Music
The Beatles - Yes It Is
Spandau Ballet - True
Grandmaster Flash - The Message
Nine Inch Nails - Hurt
The Strokes - Last Nite
Buffalo Springfield - For What It's Worth
Smashing Pumpkins - Today
Cream - I'm So Glad
Roy Orbison - It's Over
The Supremes - Where Did Our Love Go?
Alanis Morissette - You Oughta Know
Hank Williams Sr. - Your Cheatin' Heart
Linda Ronstadt - You're No Good
Eagles - Lyin' Eyes
The Replacements - I Won't
The Rolling Stones - Miss You
Waylon Jennings - You Ask Me To
Idina Menzel - Let It Go
The Commodores - Easy
Kelly Clarkson - Gone
Hank Snow - I'm Movin' On

# HEX YOUR EX VOODOO DOLL
## AN ARTS AND CRAFTS PROJECT

## MATERIALS:

- Two pieces of cloth/fabric of choice
- Marker
- Scissors
- Sewing needle and thread (unless you have a sewing machine)
- Hot-glue gun and glue stick
- A single piece of red felt cut into the shape of a heart
- A cutout of your ex's face from that picture he wouldn't let you tag him in because he didn't like the way he looked. It reminds you of how much of an asshole he really was.

- Stuffing. Optional stuffing—cut up his favorite T-shirt, you know, the one he always liked seeing you wear to bed, the one he has been begging you to return to him but you haven't because you refuse to answer or return his calls. Fuck him and his shirt.
- A piece of your ex's hair. It could be from his head, a leftover pube still in your shower or on your sheets, or beard trimmings that he could never seem to clean off your sink after shaving. Any piece of hair from him would work.

## DIRECTIONS:

1. Plug in hot-glue gun and let it heat up. Be careful when using it, because that bitch gets hot, really fast. If you burn yourself in the process, he wins. Don't let him win.

2. On the inside of your fabric pieces trace a gingerbread man pattern with the marker, making sure that they are identical. It doesn't have to be cute to be effective.

3. Place both pieces together, with the outside pieces touching, and sew 1/4 of an inch in from the border, leaving a 1-inch gap along the outside of one leg for a stuffing hole. It doesn't matter if the measurements are exact. I mean, if we are going to talk about measurements let's not forget how inaccurate he was about the length and girth of his dick when you first met. Just make sure that it's close enough to get the job done.

4. Pause for a good laugh at the inaccuracies of his measurements.

5. Clip out notches around the curves to prevent bunching.

6. Turn the sewn pieces inside out so that the hems are on the inside and the good sides of the fabric are facing the outside.

7. Trace a dick on it, so you can really get him where it hurts. You could even draw it to scale!

8. Use your T-shirt stuffing and rage stuff that fucker until it's full.

9. Close the stuffing hole by sewing it shut.

10. Use the hot-glue gun to glue the felt heart, the picture of your ex's face, and the piece of your ex's hair onto the doll. Again, be careful not to burn yourself. DON'T LET HIM WIN!

11. Spend a few minutes laughing about how ridiculous your doll looks, laugh until you cry, and then cry until you're mad.

12. Finally, when you are really mad, follow the directions on the right to complete the process of hexing your ex. The curse only works if you feel the hatred toward him for ending things the way that he has that has built up inside of you.

---

*Once all of the steps are complete you must consult your local voodoo-ologist/doctor/priestess for further guidance to cast the appropriate spell that is specific to your needs for your doll.*

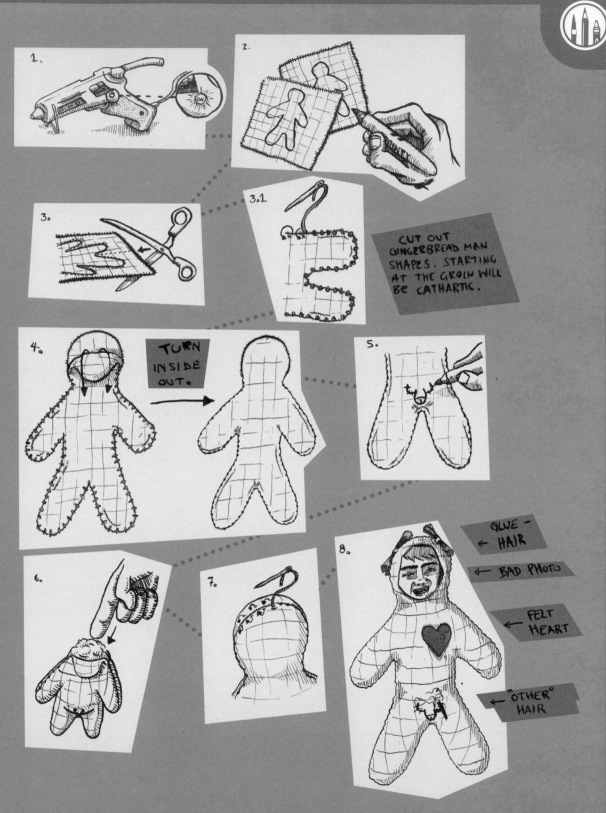

1.

2.

3.

3.1

CUT OUT GINGERBREAD MAN SHAPES. STARTING AT THE GROIN WILL BE CATHARTIC.

4.

TURN INSIDE OUT.

5.

6.

7.

8.

GLUE ← HAIR

← BAD PHOTO

FELT ← HEART

← "OTHER" HAIR

# GAMES THAT DON'T INVOLVE MY HEART

GO _UCK
YOURSEL_

Dear ~~asshole~~ Ex.

Find all the words (that describe you)
to reveal a secret message.

```
I P R C A M S O M T
S R E R R G L O W L
H I S E E A R A O J
I C O E K O T O E E
T K L P N W T R H D
H S E C A F K C U F
E W S F W L U E A R
A E F A O O D I C K
D L O O D H C T I B
E V F E R I D I O T
```

| | | | |
|---|---|---|---|
| Ass | Bitch | Creep | Dick |
| Douche | Fool | Fuckface | Idiot |
| Jerk | Loser | Moron | Prick |
| Shithead | Tool | Twatwaffle | Wanker |

Secret message:

_____

# HEARTBROKEN AT LAX
## A SHORT STORY

I walked through the airport, hating myself. Hate was a familiar thing for me to feel at airports. Well, hate's a strong word. Maybe not hate. Judgment. I was used to feeling judgmental at airports. Truth is, I was sort of a judgmental little prick.

All these stupid people and stupid stores with their stupid magazines. I always felt better than all of them. I always walked through airports in private triumph, snidely winning. But on that day, I didn't feel triumphant. As previously noted, on that morning, walking through the airport, I hated myself.

I did not hate her. I missed her. I was mad at her. I was madly in love with her. And she was madly in love with me too. No, she wasn't anymore. She had been though. For a while. A year and a half we were together. Which was a long time, considering we were both eighteen. It'd been half a year now since she'd ended it. Which was also a long time, considering I still felt like absolute shit.

I was in physical pain every day. You'd think having your heart broken would be more of a mental thing or an emotional thing, not a physical thing. But this wasn't just in my mind. My body hurt. I'd wake up and I'd wish I hadn't woken up. I wanted to be unconscious. I wanted to break stuff. Or I wanted to break myself. Or I wanted to break myself on the stuff I was breaking. I was useless. I was embarrassed. I was weak. Inexperienced and incapable. Wrong about everything. I was a loser. I certainly wasn't winning.

And so, that morning, as I walked by the people and stores and magazines, they didn't seem so stupid. Well, the magazines still did. And the stores. Also the people. Okay, everybody still seemed stupid. But the thing was, I seemed stupid too. So stupid. Cringingly stupid. Actually I seemed worse than stupid. She didn't love me anymore. And what could be worse than that? Everyone there at the airport, we were all sucking together. So who was I to judge?

Maybe if I hadn't been such a judgmental little prick, she wouldn't have left me. But if she hadn't left me, I might never have learned to stop being such a judgmental little prick.

# THE EX NICKNAME GENERATOR

Are you sick of cursing your ex's name with all of those boring, overused four-letter words? Use the chart below to create an ultra-personalized nickname for that lazy piece of dragon dick you used to call "The One."

## Day of Ex's Birth...

| | | |
|---|---|---|
| 01 egotistical | 12 slimy | 22 melodramatic |
| 02 unhygienic | 13 ungrateful | 23 visionless |
| 03 pitiful | 14 spineless | 24 inarticulate |
| 04 lazy | 15 conceited | 25 dysfunctional |
| 05 parasitic | 16 cruel | 26 maladjusted |
| 06 inbred | 17 repulsive | 27 cheap |
| 07 ignorant | 18 selfish | 28 wasteful |
| 08 obnoxious | 19 tactless | 29 heartless |
| 09 manipulative | 20 unreliable | 30 entitled |
| 10 pretentious | 21 abusive | 31 superficial |
| 11 brainless | | |

## Month of Ex's Birth...

| | |
|---|---|
| January | cold-hearted |
| February | mouth-breathing |
| March | boot-licking |
| April | attention-starved |
| May | oxygen-depleting |
| June | self-serving |
| July | blood-sucking |
| August | two-faced |
| September | double-dealing |
| October | crazy-eyed |
| November | foul-mouthed |
| December | soul-crushing |

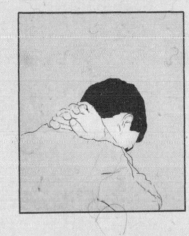

## First Letter of Ex's Name...

| | | |
|---|---|---|
| **A assreek | J jock itch | S shit streak |
| B bowel sack | K knife wound | T toilet brush |
| C cockroach | L litter box | U urinal cake |
| D demonspawn | M muff lint | V vomit rag |
| E earwig | N nightmare | W wank stain |
| F fuckweasel | O oxball | X xenomorph |
| G gastropod | P piss bucket | Y yak bag |
| H hellspit | Q quicksand | Z zoo toxin |
| I icicle | R rat pellet | |

**EXAMPLE:**
Dave, DOB: April 16th
*Cruel attention-starved demon spawn*

# AND NOW I WILL CALL YOU...

Don't get mad, get creative! Use all your pent up anger and let it out on your exes old and new. Use the chart to the left and give them the nicknames they deserve (we know you still secretly remember their birthday).

EX #1: _____

EX #2: _____

EX #3: _____

EX #4: _____

EX #5: _____

EX #6: _____

EX #7: _____

EX #8: _____

EX #9: _____

EX #10: _____

# YOU SAID YOU NEEDED SPACE _ _ _ _

... so here's a whole bunch of them! Just ask a friend for the types of words indicated below the lines, and use their answers to fill in the blank spaces in the stories (something your garbage liar of an ex was just never able to convincingly accomplish). Once you've filled in all the missing words, read the story aloud... it'll most likely sound completely ridiculous, and yet somehow still make more sense than some of the horsesh*t your ex seemed to expect you to believe. Have (as much) fun (as possible from the couch you haven't moved away from in three days!)

**Instructions:**
**How to Play!**

Dear _ _ _ _ ,

Do you remember the time we got into a fight and you threw out
all my _____ ?
    (plural noun)
That was shitty. You know what was even more shitty? When you
took my_____ and my_____ and threw **them** across the _____ . I
        (noun)            (noun)                              (noun)
waited for_____hours on Black Friday for that _____. And
        (number)                                (noun)
just like that_____it was gone.
            (onomatopoeia)

Remember when we took a trip to_____? I _____
                    (location)        (past tense verb)
that trip. I even went on a _____excursion because I knew you
                            (noun)
wanted to...and I hate _____! Yeah you still owe me_____from
                        (plural noun)                      (noun)
that trip.

The only thing you had going for you was your dog.

_____ is more loyal, _____, and _____
  (name)                      (adjective)        (adjective)
than you'll ever be.

Basically I just wanted you to know that I _____ you. I
                                            (verb)

mentally throw a dart at your _____ every time I think of
                                (noun)

you and that _____ from _____.
              (noun)       (location)

Love (Jt hate),

_____
  (name)

P.S. I told your mom that you _____
                              (verb)

in your sleep.

     P.S.S. My grandma (or as you call her, _____) thinks
                                             (name)

  you're _____.
       (adjective)

XXXX you
(verb)

I was _____ a _____ whom I met at _____. It was a _____
    (verb) (occupation)                (place)           (adjective)
experience for both of us. For hours on end we would _____ and
                                              (verb)
_____. We both enjoyed _____ and watching
(verb)                   (type of food)
_____. I thought we were _____ for each
(type of entertainment)                (superlative)
other. I was ready for _____. Until one day I discovered he/she
                   (noun)
was _____ with other _____! I was so _____ and
   (verb)         (plural noun)          (emotive verb)
_____ that I swore I'd _____ him/her. Instead I
(emotive verb)            (criminal act)
_____ his/her _____ bright _____!
(past tense verb)     (body part)      (color)
You know what they say:

"_____..."
(favorite line from a book, song, or movie)

# KARMA SUTRA

## POSITIONS THAT WILL RESULT IN GOOD KARMA

### ① THE SLUGGER

The BROKEN HEARTED is wearing boxing gloves, hitting a punching bag with a photo of their ex stuck to it. Clearly exhausted and a sweaty mess, but still going at it and screaming while punching.

### ② THE TUMBLING WHEELBARROW

The BROKEN HEARTED has pushed a wheelbarrow filled with the HEARTBREAKER's possessions down a hill, and it is tumbling away—scattering its contents all over the hillside.

## POSITIONS THAT WILL PROBABLY RESULT IN BAD KARMA

###  THE TROLL

The BROKEN HEARTED sat at a computer, looking at their ex's happy posts, and furiously typing snide comments.

### ④ THE BRIDGE

The BROKEN HEARTED stands in the middle of a busy bridge, shouting at the top of their lungs about how much they hate their ex. The only closure here will be traffic-related.

# Breakup Cookie
## RECIPE

**STEP 1**

BUY A ROLL OF COOKIE DOUGH AND MOLD IT INTO INDIVIDUAL COOKIE SHAPES ON A TRAY.

**STEP 2**

PRE-HEAT YOUR OVEN TO THE HIGHEST POSSIBLE TEMPERATURE.

**STEP 3**

INSERT TRAY OF COOKIES INTO OVEN.

**STEP 4**

BAKE THE SHIT OUT OF THE COOKIES UNTIL THEY BURN TO A CRISP.

**STEP 5**

REMOVE FROM OVEN AND LET THE COOKIES COOL.

**STEP 6**

DRINK A BOTTLE OF WHISKEY AND THROW BURNED COOKIES INTO A RIVER WHILE YOU SCREAM OBSCENITIES.

FLOUR
SUGAR
BUTTER
WHISKEY
MILK

# THINGS THAT REMIND ME OF MY EX
## WORD SEARCH

```
D V K S L I A M E S S A M L L A Y L P E R F A
S E I N W S P O T H O L E S W T F X S A E W E
A K D R A P A P P L C O T E D D E Z A R L E Z
T V S A X A P E E S A C D Q O J X C C K E T F
U D K K G M E X B O L M O R N I N G P E O P L
R F I N G E R N A I L S O N B L A C K B O A R
D G C A T M C A R V W O C E V R A B R E X P A
A V K A R A U M R F A E U R X E R T G Z D E A
Y O I H R I T A F T I K I D A T A V R X A R X
M I N D I L S O R R T F G A C P B A Q A R D R
O L G P O S A F K D I H S F R H I F H M F O Z
R G S R F I N O M R N V I S D G E N R H E F J
N B E D O G D R E G G Q H K E E A W G L A U I
I D A T H U L Y F A H D I G R T T R E F L A R
N O T A H R E T H E W O R D M O I S T R O N G
G I S D S T M S V N R U H J F G A V R V S R O
C T O N E R O G U G I B A F T K A D I L O N K
O B N O K U N N F D O L F H R I V O K L A K F
N R P R Q E J I X V O E F D O R C A B I T H P
S P L E G R U K U F V P U N G E R S T E L O L
T F A R T T I A S L I A M E M A P S K M R L A
R T N E R O C E R C Q R G F R H O J Y K Y E O
U O E A B E E U M V R K U A V R S A S H F T U
C L S R A N K Q U T A I N G E R I M G F L A B
T O O T H P A S T E A N D O R A N G E J U I C
I A E F U T H O T T Y G L O V O R Q U S O V N
O N F R A C N A E L C N O T I H S D R I B R A
```

ROADKILL

SPORKS

TOOTHPASTE AND ORANGE JUICE

PAPER CUTS AND LEMON JUICE

SCRAPING FORKS

SATURDAY MORNING CONSTRUCTION

FINGERNAILS ON BLACKBOARD

SQUEAKING STYROFOAM

KIDS KICKING SEATS ON PLANES

WET PAPER

LOUD CHEWERS

THE WORD *MOIST*

MORNING PEOPLE

SPAM EMAILS

CALL WAITING

POTHOLES

# GLOSSARY OF EXES

### THE CHRISTOPHER COLUMBUS

Convinces you that you are exotic uncharted territory that only they are capable of discovering. Then they leave and you discover you have diseases that you didn't have before.

### THE DAVID COPPERFIELD

Flamboyant illusionist. The relationship is all smoke and mirrors and then they just disappear ... Then unfortunately reappear, usually at the most inopportune time. Prone to excessive use of eyeliner.

### THE EDMUND HILLARY

Once they've conquered you they're off on a new adventure. Possibly missing the odd finger or toe.

### THE EVEL KNIEVEL

Charismatic daredevil who will take you along for the ride, but before you know it, the whole thing goes up in smoke and you go down in flames.

### THE F. SCOTT FITZGERALD

Relies on your relationship for artistic material but does not afford you the same courtesy. Later will decry you as crazy and possibly have you committed.

• *Fitzgeralded* (verb) The act of being mistaken as crazy (when you are clearly just misunderstood) and being institutionalized due to your ex's exceptional storytelling ability.

　　Example: "But Doctor, I'm not crazy; I've just been Fitzgeralded."

### THE HOUDINI

Captivating. Just when you think you've got the relationship locked down, they escape.

### THE JIMMY HOFFA

Loud and driven with acquaintances of dubious provenance. Pulls the most epic disappearing trick of all time. Often confused with the David Copperfield, this one does not reappear. Ever. Also, has no affinity for eyeliner.

### THE LANCE ARMSTRONG

You support them through their lowest, but when it's time for them to do the same, they're on their bike. Notorious for wearing far too much lycra.

### THE NOAH

Has been with two of everything, so don't even bother unless you are a unicorn.

### THE SHRÖDINGER

In the event that the relationship was never defined, it can neither be current or over. Ergo, the other person is a shrödinger, neither your partner nor your ex.

# 6
# BARGAINING

When it comes to rekindling your love, absolutely nothing is off limits. As they say—go big or go home...alone.

**This is the BARGAINING chapter**—or the art of winning them back while avoiding a restraining order.

**Did you know that 50% of all breakups result in permanent separation?**

Dear Broken Hearted,

Most programs will tell you to "just be yourself and hope for the best" to get your ex back. **But not the...**

**Here at the EX-TO-BEST PROGRAM, we'll teach you how to bargain your way back to any ex just by following a few simple steps! Here's a taste of what you can expect to learn from us:**

**Admit Faults:**
Confession is good for the soul. And, most important, it earns you points with your ex. So, open up about stealing toilet paper from work or the time you ran over the neighbor's cat, and your ex will be primed to believe whatever you say.

**Cater to Their Fears:**
Make sure to say how much you love that one physical attribute they're self-conscious about (big nose, small hands, etc.). Casually mention how that's what makes them special. Everyone else will seem shallow in comparison.

**Offer a Great Deal:**
Concede to them winning all arguments for a period of no less than one year, and promise to change at least two aspects of your personality or habits they have always found annoying. It will be impossible for them to decline your proposition.

**Grab Them By the Stomach:**
Enroll in a cooking class, and make sure to learn how to cook every single one of your ex's favorite dishes to perfection. Then send them some "leftovers," as you would any other "friend."

**FOMO (Fear of Missing Out):**
Cultivate the impression that you may not be on the market much longer. Pointing out another's romantic interest in you makes you considerably more attractive to your ex.

**Deadline Discount:**
The best strategy is to maximize your perceived value. If you let your ex think they can get a discount whenever they want, you will cheapen the reputation of your brand. Think quality. Put a timeframe on the discount to limit availability.
***And much, much more!!!***

**The first 50 purchases of this program will also get our exclusive booklet *"10 Ways to Look Good by Admitting Faults: The Art of the Humble Brag,"* completely free of charge!**

**And, for today only, this relationship rescue package, worth $1,550, is yours for a special reduced rate. That's right. If you act now, this God-sent gift can be yours for just $500! What are you waiting for?**

Buy the EX-TO-BEST PROGRAM now and get your well-deserved romantic bliss delivered to you by express mail!

It's almost a giveaway, but we have your best interests at heart.

Plus...
If after the complimentary period of two weeks you still haven't gotten a date out of your ex, just send all the materials back and we'll refund all your money. You read it correctly, a 100% money back guarantee! That's how sure we are that this program changes lives.

Don't be a statistic. Be moderately happy with someone who's broken up with you, at least once before, forever!

Sincerely,

P. Smith, President of Ex-to-Best Inc.

**P.S. If everything else fails, we'll teach you how to hack into your ex's computer and email their new love interest some armpit porn from their account "by mistake."**

Hey, it's me.
I think I left my heart at your place.
Kinda need it.
If you haven't thrown it in the trash yet,
it should be somewhere on the floor,
scattered into pieces.

# GOOD REASONS TO CALL YOUR EX

- You just missed a call from a private number and you swear it was from them. How strange.

- To give them a heads-up before you go out to lunch with their mom and/or best friend.

- To ask them to come over and open a particularly difficult jar of olives that you absolutely need for dinner that night.

- To check when the last time you had sex was so you don't tell the wrong person you're "late."

- To offer them coupons for their favorite restaurant that you "just happened" to get in the mail.

- The kids want to see them.

- To ask them for the Wi-Fi password because you forgot it, and have some very urgent work emails to send at 11:47 on a Friday night.

- To get help with your tax returns, because they were always so much better than you at that.

- You "accidentally" butt dialed them while singing your couple song in the car.

- "Hey! What's the red triangle flashing light on my dash mean?"

- You find some of her clothes as you fold the laundry in your new bachelor pad. You must have just grabbed a pile of clothes without thinking when you left.

- The latest Marvel movie is coming out next week, and you bought the last two opening-night tickets before the relationship crashed. You know they never buy anything in advance, and since they got you hooked on these films, you figured it would only make sense for them to tag along.

- Your bathroom drain is clogged because of their hair. They should totally have to come and clean it out. Ewwww.

- You found their limited-edition Death Cab for Cutie CD, still wrapped in plastic, in your CD collection. You let them know you are tempted to open it to have a listen.

- The dog, of which you have custody, is missing them.

# LIMERICKS

I'm so very eager to please,

We can try that weird thing with bees!

Slather me in honey,

So sticky and runny

That'll double our housecleaning fees!

For my lost love I am yearning,

I dream to see her returning,

So I wrote "You're my life,"

On my arm with a knife,

But she said she just found it concerning.

# NOT ENOUGH
## A POEM

Today I wore too much makeup,
but it was not enough to make me feel pretty.

Today I dressed in too many layers,
but it was not enough to keep me warm.

Today I said, "I love you," too many times,
but it was not enough to make you stay.

Tonight I'll have too many pillows in the bed,
but it will not be enough to bring me comfort.

Tomorrow I will be ugly, cold, and alone,
but it will not be enough to stop me
from trying again.

TEARS
OF
REGRET

# 7

# DEPRESSION

All hope is lost. They won't take you back and you'll never find love again. Time to accept your fate: to die alone and be eaten by your cats who probably don't love you either.

**This is the DEPRESSION chapter**—or the art of filling the gaping hole in your heart with ice cream and rom-coms.

How can I be clinically depressed if my blood type is B positive?

# BROKEN HEARTED

## WORD SEARCH

```
        Y H R F            N E B M
      B K Q E A U        G F D Y D C
    C S F W I A V J      B S D R E A R Y
    B A O O N H C R U D L A B R T F Y H L N
  E R T D M P A E G T B Y Y O R D G D A E P N
G H E A O E E H N E N A L S A O N D N K Y O N Z
B G Z S S W P I O W L O C E Z I D O C M I H G L
C R N T E A Y R O N H F H H B P I I A T N N U U
O I T R M R D R E C Y N M B E T R N A O M F U O
N E L O C I R E N S W L O W C T O C I X N J T M
Z F G P S O F A M O S S X I S E I T L R G N F R
  L T H S G L F D P I E L C S F C G U A E K E
  R I E K E H P E F T F D Y I E N O T D A T R
  E S M O C R U D F Y K T J R M K N F F Z
    S T R M L M A K P R E E C Q O R I C
    E L C F O I H O D T O Y P E R I
    N E R B S M V A J R S M G D
      T S U M E E Q G E M X E
      F S S H R N D A L G
      U C H A U C K A
      L N E S F M
      V G D A
      J D
```

| | |
|---|---|
| AFFLICTION | HEARTACHE |
| ANGRY | INSOMNIA |
| CATASTROPHE | LISTLESS |
| CHEATER | LOSER |
| CON | MELANCHOLY |
| CRUSHED | MIFFED |
| CRYING | MORTIFICATION |
| DAMAGED | MOURNFUL |
| DEJECTION | PHONY |
| DEPRESSED | RESENTFUL |
| DESPONDENT | SAD |
| DOWNHEARTED | SCAMMER |
| DREARY | SOBBING |
| EMPTY | SORROW |
| GRIEF | SORRY |
| GRIFTER | STRICKEN |

if Romance is dead

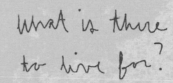

what is there to live for?

# COMPLETELY
## A POEM

Take back the lunches
and the dinners
all the fuzzy claw game winners
take the gifts
and all their bows
take each and every note
take back the sweet and sour words
take back the painting of the birds
take back the trips and all the sights
all the drives and all the flights
take back the songs
and all the wrongs
you can even take the rights
along with every late, late night
good and bad
happy or sad
take everything we had
take back the tea
the countless movies
every breakfast
and all the rest of
the things we did
in bed
take the sunset skies
we'd stop our lives
to see from docks
on mountain tops
barefoot on the many shores
take all that isn't anymore
take all the photos and the memories
and anything left in between
I only wanted you

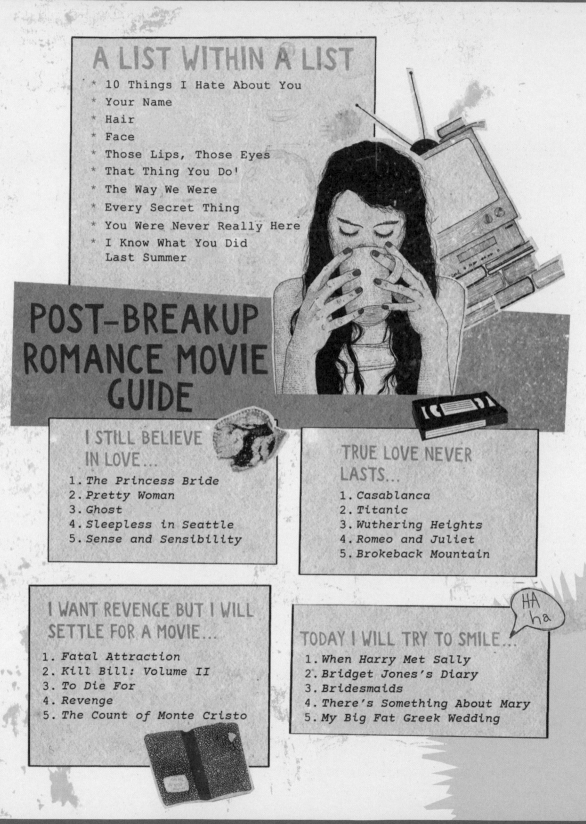

## A LIST WITHIN A LIST

* 10 Things I Hate About You
* Your Name
* Hair
* Face
* Those Lips, Those Eyes
* That Thing You Do!
* The Way We Were
* Every Secret Thing
* You Were Never Really Here
* I Know What You Did
  Last Summer

# POST-BREAKUP ROMANCE MOVIE GUIDE

### I STILL BELIEVE IN LOVE...

1. *The Princess Bride*
2. *Pretty Woman*
3. *Ghost*
4. *Sleepless in Seattle*
5. *Sense and Sensibility*

### TRUE LOVE NEVER LASTS...

1. *Casablanca*
2. *Titanic*
3. *Wuthering Heights*
4. *Romeo and Juliet*
5. *Brokeback Mountain*

### I WANT REVENGE BUT I WILL SETTLE FOR A MOVIE...

1. *Fatal Attraction*
2. *Kill Bill: Volume II*
3. *To Die For*
4. *Revenge*
5. *The Count of Monte Cristo*

### TODAY I WILL TRY TO SMILE...

1. *When Harry Met Sally*
2. *Bridget Jones's Diary*
3. *Bridesmaids*
4. *There's Something About Mary*
5. *My Big Fat Greek Wedding*

# ☰ Breakup Thesaurus

**synonyms** | broken hearted 🔍

*top results for*

## broken hearted *(name)*

♥ Cheesy Ballads Playlist Creator

♥ Conscientious Objector of Happy Couples

♥ Talented Social Media Stalker

♥ Cell Phone Silence Subtext Interpreter

♥ Reluctant Holder of Duvet Monopoly

♥ Love Song Fact-Checker

♥ Love Letter Arsonist

♥ Orgasm Soloist

♥ Couch Nudist

♥ Professional Tissue User

♥ Waterproof Mascara Enthusiast

♥ Tear-Facial Expert

♥ Soulmate Agnostic

♥ Fractured Myocardium Sufferer

♥ Sympathy-Looks Collector

♥ Meal-for-One Specialist

♥ Ice Cream Connoisseur

♥ Felony Waiting to Happen

♥ Repeat Text Offender

♥ Compulsive Online Shopper

♥ Romantic Comedies Critic

♥ Scriber of Bad Verse

♥ Person Who Eats Unimaginable Amounts of Chocolate While Still in Denial about the Paper Wrapper Evidence in the Trash

*Click here to see all 57,532 results*

# THE ORIGAMI GUIDE TO HEARTBREAK

## 1.

Hearts always start out smooth, clean, and unblemished...

## 2.

But then you meet someone, and it does a little flip-flop.

## 3.

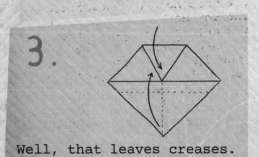

Well, that leaves creases.

## 4.

But you kind of like the way the change feels, so you carry on.

## 5.

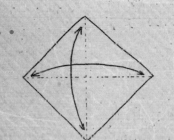

Letting your heart be shaped and manipulated...

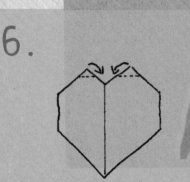

**6.**

...until it becomes something quite unlike what is was before.

**8.**

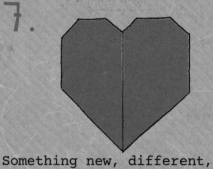

**7.**

Something new, different, intricate. Something better. And that's how it is...

...until the fucker tears it to shreds.

l o v e is shit......

# Rx

Tapering Schedule for
## "Thoughts of Your Ex"

FRIEND-ZONED
TABLETS

Friend-Zoned
Tablets $7.00

**Patient #:** *4205551*

**Duration of Rehabilitation Process:** *6 months to 1 year*

**Type of Care:** *Outpatient*

The first step is accepting your addiction and making the decision to overcome it.

JUST
CRUSH

Jealousy
Pills

## PRECAUTIONS:

- Symptoms may become worse if THOUGHTS OF YOUR EX are ceased abruptly. You may experience stress rash, mood swings, loss of appetite, increased appetite, the desire to watch daytime TV, insomnia, sleepiness, and confusion.

- YOUR DOSE SHOULD BE GRADUALLY TAPERED to decrease the risk of added side effects.

- If you feel the urge to go back to using THOUGHTS OF YOUR EX during this process, immediately call a friend or family member from your support group and tell them to talk some sense into you.

Heartbreak
Solution
mend that broken
heart with our
new healing sol

# TAPERING SCHEDULE:

Week 1    Removing THOUGHTS OF YOUR EX from Your Life
This includes, but is not limited to:

- Boxing up all of your ex's clothing, except for a single article that you are to wear while you scroll through their social media for 15 minutes every 8 hours.
- Deleting all pictures featuring both of you, even if only part of one of your ex's limbs is visible in the frame, at the rate of no less than 10 every 24 hours.
- Deleting your ex's phone number from your cellular device and keeping it at a minimum distance of 6 feet, if you have the number memorized.
- Changing the coordinates for your ex's house on your GPS device to your local gym.

Week 2    Taking Care of Yourself

- Take 1 to 2 naps a day, as needed. At least, while you're sleeping you're not having THOUGHTS OF YOUR EX.
- Make sure to include all comfort-food groups in your meals: chocolate, ice cream, bread, and fried foods.
- Drink plenty of alcohol-rich fluids in the company of friends but never while alone and watching romantic comedies.
- Wear comfortable clothes that don't require more than 1 wash per week.

Week 3 to 52    The Hard Part

- Gradually reduce all aforementioned behaviors, at your own pace, and make sure to ask for help if you feel yourself slipping back into "week 1 conduct."
- We advise deleting all social media accounts before week 5 to assure mental stability.

Good Luck!

Dr. Bre Cup

-General-
LoveSickness
-Capsules-

LoveSickness
Capsules
$10.50

# RECIPE FOR a

## Ingredients / BASIC VERSION

1 TSP. OF EMOTIONAL ANGER

1 1/4 TSP. OF UNHAPPINESS

3 TBSP. OF *BROKEN LOYALTY*

2 C. OF LIES AND DECEIT

1 1/4 C. OF ANXIETY

+ + + + OF PLAUSIBLE THERAPY VISITS

## Ingredients / LARGER VERSION

USE SAME AS BEFORE BUT ADD:

LONELINESS + 13 TBSP. OF NONCHALANCE + AN OUNCE OF EMPATHY + *99% PROOF* REGRET

# BRKEN HEART

## To garnish:

A PINCH OF SALT

+

4 SOUR GRAPES

+

WHISKEY

1 SHOT

ADD MORE OR LESS ACCORDING TO TASTE

## Recipe:

**1.** ADD ALL INGREDIENTS (AS MANY VARIATIONS) IN A LARGE MIXING BOWL.

**2.** MIX WITH A COLD SPATULA TO REFLECT THE LITERAL COLD, DEAD HEART IN FRONT OF YOU.

**3.** SCOOP MIXTURE INTO A METAL TRAY.

**4.** ADD GARNISHES ACCORDING TO PENT-UP EMOTIONS.

5 DAYS

**5.** PLACE TRAY IN THE FRIDGE.

**6.** DRINK WINE AND WALLOW.

**7.** DON'T REMOVE THE TRAY UNTIL YOU FEEL YOUR COLD HEART BEATING AGAIN.

**8.** ONCE YOUR MOJO AND FEELINGS HAVE BEEN RESTORED, TAKE OUT MIXTURE AND TOSS IT.

**9. You won't need it anymore.**

# 8
# ACCEPTANCE

Maybe you've found some closure, or maybe you've realized you're better off without them. Either way, you've dragged yourself through the tunnel of love and emerged, blinking, into the light.

**This is the ACCEPTANCE chapter**—or the art of moving on.

# ACCEPTANCE YOGA

*You've survived the breakup! These yoga poses will increase your flexibility and strengthen your core for stability in the brave new world!*

a. **Hindsight Stance**—Your feet are firmly planted, your back is strong, and your ex looks best in your rearview mirror.

b. **Regrets, My Ass**—To anyone suggesting you should doubt yourself or lose sight of your center, a fart is the only appropriate response.

c. **Full-Body Smiley Face**—You are open to a new relationship, and your body just can't stop smiling. You're so ready for this! The breakup was the best thing that ever happened to you. Yay!

d. **Sweet Liberty Stance**—You're done being a huddled mass. Reclaim the three vital elements you lost during your relationship—strength, balance, and freedom. You'll carry a torch again when you're ready, and not a moment sooner.

e. **Downward Toes**—Repeat after me: "The only person I'll bend over backward for today is myself."

f. **Bingewatchavasana**—You finally control the remote, and you and your shows have a lot of catching up to do. Meow.

g. **Snuggle Stance**—Lovers come and go, but the one heart you can always count on has been with you all along, waiting for you to recognize your own value. Wrap your lovin' arms around yourself—you really do give the best hugs.

h. **Water Under the Bridge**—The stupid shit your ex pulled no longer bothers you! You're all about building new bridges and letting the stress float away.

# GET BACK OUT THERE!

### →CHECKLIST←

☐ DEEP BREATH

☐ GET RID OF ALL MEMORIES OF X

☐ SCRUB OIL & DESPERATION FROM FACE

☐ THE "NEW ME"!!!

   ☐ REMOVE ALL OVERGROWN, UNWANTED BODY HAIR

   ☐ MAX OUT CREDIT CARD FOR NEW WARDROBE

☐ BINGE ON ROMANTIC COMEDIES FOR TIPS & STRATEGIES

☐ BRUSH UP ON WHAT'S ~~"HIP & WITH IT"~~
   ↳ OUTDATED... BUT ANYWAY!

☐ SUPERHERO POSE TO BOOST CONFIDENCE!

☐ START RADICALLY BIZARRE NEW HOBBIES (NEW TALKING POINTS!)

"HOW TO BE A MERMAID IN 7 DAYS"

☐ DEEEEP BREATH!!!

☐ GET. BACK. OUT. THERE.

# OUR SOULS ARE RESILIENT
## A SHORT STORY

I didn't hate you when we broke up. I couldn't bear to do so. You and I spent nearly six years together—in arguments, in twisted sheets, at awkward family gatherings. We made each other happy, through most of it, and that was enough. Until it wasn't anymore.

When we met, our lives collided. I remember the first time I said "hello." I learned your name and the color of your eyes. You uncovered what made me nervous. The wind was warm, the stars were out. You kissed me because my hands were shaking. I woke up wishing I was holding your hand.

It was raining when I first told you that I loved you. I could have sworn my heart beat in rhythm with the raindrops. We dried off beside the fire. You told me stories. Fairy tales, mostly.

Years slipped by. You said it felt like we were old people already, reminiscing about the past, as though there was nothing in the present to sustain us. You never mentioned the future.

When you ended it the sun was shining. I cut through the park back to my place and could smell the cherry blossoms. I walked with aching legs and collapsed to the floor.

For months, I was convinced that you had made a mistake. That you only needed some time to think things over and, soon enough, you would miss me. Because what else did we have but each other? What else did I have but you?

If we were different people, it might have worked out. In some other universe, with stars in the sea and oceans in the sky, maybe we held hands until the day we died. But that's not what happened.

It hurts a lot more often than I'm prepared to admit, but even so, my heart still beats. Sometimes with the rhythm of the raindrops, but mostly with the rhythm of other things. Like melodies and footsteps, and someone else's breathing.

"Our souls are resilient," was something a stranger I tried to love once said to me. I don't remember their name, or their face, or even where we met, but those four words have haunted me.

I have everything else but you. And eventually, that will be okay. Won't it?

# THE ~~ACCEPTANCE~~ LETTER

~~[Broken Hearted]~~, Dear Heartbreaker,

I'll get straight to the point:

I ~~want to break up.~~

~~You probably don't know all the~~
~~reasons why I want to - or maybe you~~
~~do. Honestly, all I used to think is~~
~~I wouldn't know how I'd live without~~
~~you. But as it turns out, I need to~~
~~live without~~ you. ~~The fights, the~~
~~resentment, and the time spent~~
~~growing apart... This was never~~
~~going to work with you. We have too~~
~~much holding us down, and nothing in~~
~~common. And... I don't know if I~~
~~love you anymore. There's nothing~~
~~that you, I, or we can do to bring~~
~~us back. I thought I'd just save you~~
~~the trouble and get it over with.~~
~~There isn't anything we can do.~~
~~We're just not meant to be together.~~

~~I'm breaking up with you.~~

~~I'm sorry.~~

~~[Heartbreaker]~~

FROM,
THE FORMERLY ^ BROKEN HEARTED

# MY EX IS WORSE THAN YOURS...
## A BOARD GAME

winner

winner

winner

winner

start

start

start

start

**RULES**
**2 to 4 players. You will need: Coins, die.**

Put coins on the starting circles. Roll die and read the statement in Roll 1 box according to the number on the die. Any player who can answer yes to the statement move their coin one step. Roll the die again and read the statement in the Roll 2 box according to the number on the die. If no one has reached the winner square by the time you finish the Roll 6 box, start over with the Roll 1 box. Continue until someone has reached the winner square.

ROLL 1
1. My ex cheated on me
2. My ex didn't break up with me face-to-face
3. I had to do my ex's laundry
4. My ex kept the house/apartment
5. My ex took the dog/cat
6. My ex didn't chew with his/her mouth closed

ROLL 2
1. My ex slept with my best friend
2. My ex hit on my sister/brother
3. My ex broke up via text message
4. My ex never cooked dinner for me
5. My ex went on vacation without me
6. My ex disliked my friends

ROLL 3
1. My ex called me names
2. My ex changed his/her Facebook status to single before breaking up with me
3. My ex threw my things through the window
4. My ex took our mutual friends
5. My ex is a slob
6. My ex took me for granted

ROLL 4
1. My ex always flirted with the waiter when we went out
2. My ex had bad personal hygiene
3. My mom never liked my ex
4. My ex never said he/she loved me
5. My ex never let me pick the movie
6. My ex never cleaned the bathroom

ROLL 5
1. My ex has commitment issues
2. My ex needs therapy
3. My ex trolls me online
4. My ex still calls my mom
5. My ex cheated on me with a work colleague
6. My ex is a liar

ROLL 6
1. My ex didn't give back his/her ring
2. My ex is already seeing someone new
3. My ex called me fat
4. My ex is a control freak
5. My ex turned my friends against me
6. My ex used me for my money

When exiting the joint place of residence, do so quickly, following the advice of your friends and family and leaving all tainted items behind. Your relationship will now be behind you.

I finally kicked my habit of you.

I'll always be a recovering "you-addict," but at least I don't need you to get through the day anymore.

It took me a long time to see the destruction you brought into my life. For months, all I could think about was the good moments; the highs you gave me. And I wanted so much to have you again—one last time—just to take the edge off. But I knew that even after just one dose, I'd be back to the same obsessive behavior as before—the constant texting, the endless questions, and the inescapable feeling of complete emptiness.

The new guy was just another vice—a rebound—keeping me from craving you so much, but it worked. Now, I can even say your name without hating you.

You're a chapter of my book I won't delete but rather close. And I can't wait to start writing a new one.

SCAN FOR A COMPLETE
BREAKDOWN OF CREDITS
AND RESOURCES

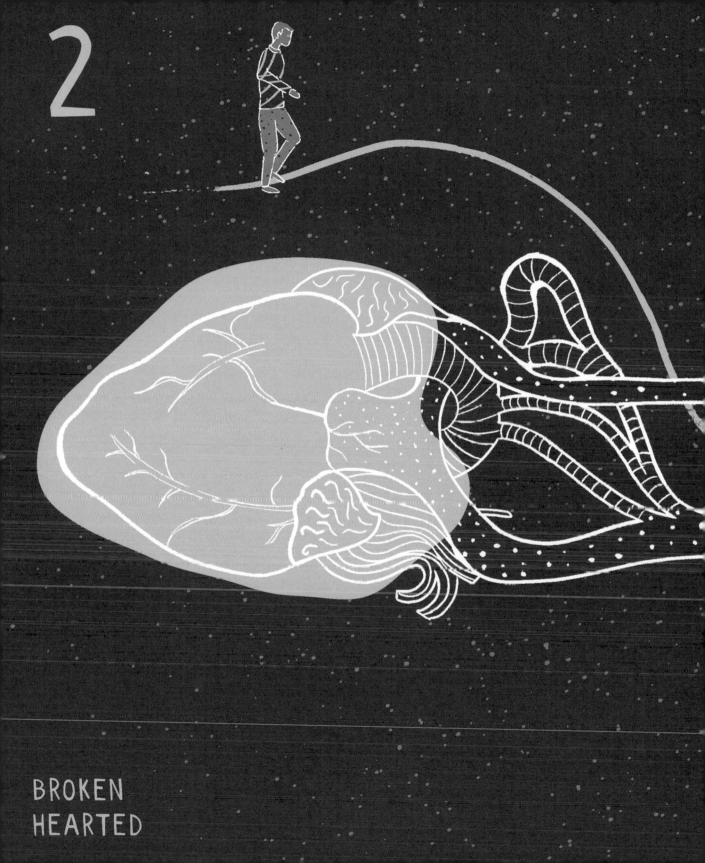

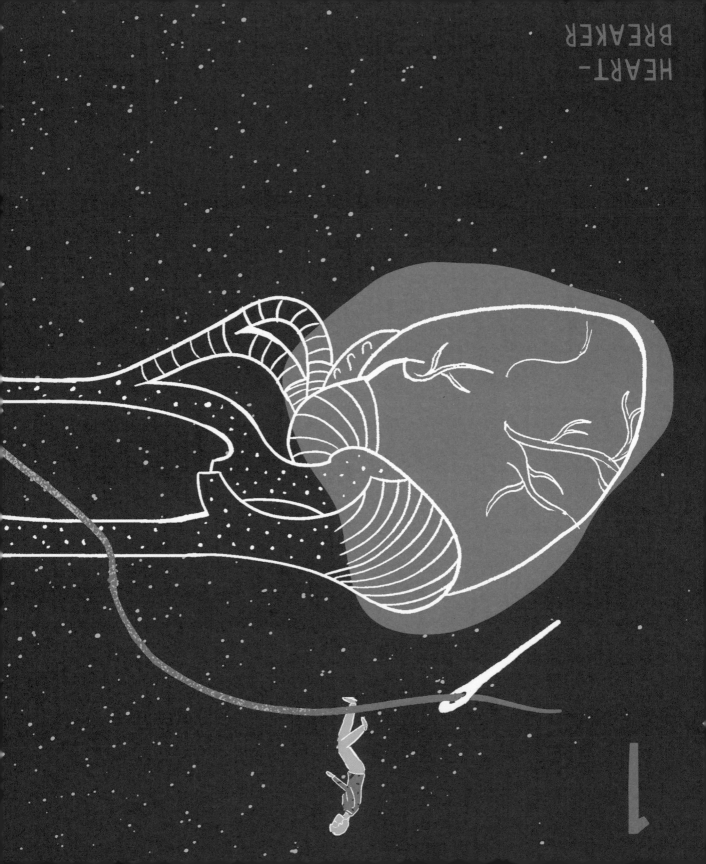

1

SCAN FOR A COMPLETE
BREAKDOWN OF CREDITS
AND RESOURCES

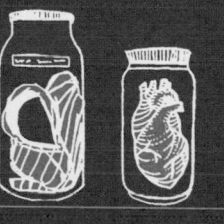
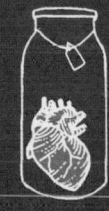

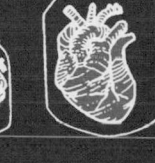
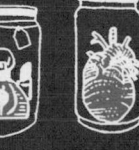

## Navel-Gazing Hedgehog:

Visualize the quills spreading from your back, protecting you from reality while you grunt and squeal your way to the center of your problems. If you can't find the core of your issues here, it's a good bet you don't really have any.

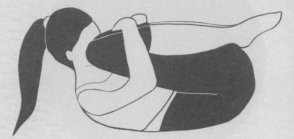

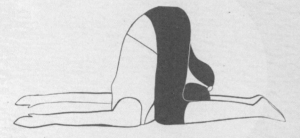

## A Not-So-Fresh Perspective:

Your lover has accused you of having your head up your ass. Proving this to be physically impossible is a step toward realizing they must not have meant all those other terrible things they said, either.

## Extended Peek-a-Boo:

You made your boo disappear, but this tried-and-true method just might bring them back! At the very least, it will prevent you from seeing that you are, in fact, alone.

She went out on the beer run, marveling at how the neighborhood was frozen in a previous era, like a dragonfly in amber. By the time she returned, the first friends had arrived. It was the nightly party, everyone loud and wasted. She spent the next few hours shouting until her voice was hoarse, choking on cigarette smoke, astonished by the fact that her old friends were so unappealing.

As morning came and everyone else staggered off to their lairs, Brad's best friend Chaz, who believed that armpit fart noises were the soul of wit, vomited prolifically on the bed. There was nowhere to sleep. Brad had taken the only comfortable alternative, the sofa with its assortment of mysterious, unpleasant odors, so Maya was relegated to sleeping upright in the chair with the sprung springs, as she had so many times in the past.

When dawn broke, Brad awoke and staggered over to her, breathing his sour breath in her face and asking for a blowjob.

She pretended to be asleep, so he returned to the sofa and fell asleep again.

Maya had originally planned to somehow break the system, to find a way for her and Brad to be together forever. Suddenly hungry, she reached for a soggy slice of cheap, rubbery pizza, and as she ate, she fantasized about freshly baked bran muffins, a run in the park, and a night of crafting with peaceful, clever companions.

# DENIAL YOGA

So you've said the relationship is over, but you didn't mean it!
Use these specially designed yoga poses to keep yourself busy
while you wait for your ex to take you back.

## Downward-Facing Ostrich:

This highly versatile pose is perfect at the beach, in the bathroom, or any time you need to bury your feelings deep between the pillows. Plus, it helps keep muscle memory sharp for your lover's inevitable return! You'll want to strike this pose the minute they slam the door!

## Arbor-trary Listening:

Who says you need to stand on your own two feet? This pose will make you strong like a sapling in the wind—bent, not broken! With your hands placed firmly over your ears, all those depressing declarations and unsolicited advice will sound like a gentle breeze through your branches. After all, if a relationship fails but you can't hear it, are you actually broken up?

the things we say and never feel
are worse than
the things we feel and never say

# DRAW YOUR FUTURE, HAPPY LIFE TOGETHER!

## BREAKUP? WHAT BREAKUP?!

Cut up some photos and paste your faces below.
Then draw the rest of this scene for your happy future together!

your photo here

their photo here

Who knows? This could be next year's holiday card!

Find | Near | Log In | Sign Up

# My Newfound Single Life ★★★★☆
4 Reviews

☆ Write A Review

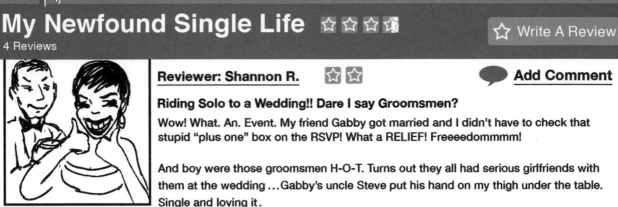

**Reviewer: Shannon R.** ☆☆     💬 **Add Comment**

**Riding Solo to a Wedding!! Dare I say Groomsmen?**

Wow! What. An. Event. My friend Gabby got married and I didn't have to check that stupid "plus one" box on the RSVP! What a RELIEF! Freeeedommmm!

And boy were those groomsmen H-O-T. Turns out they all had serious girlfriends with them at the wedding…Gabby's uncle Steve put his hand on my thigh under the table. Single and loving it.

**Reviewer: Nicole M.**      💬 **Add Comment**

**Swipe Right or GO HOME!**

I'm newly single and ready to mingle, baby. Most of my friends are in long-term relationships…or have kids already. So dating apps…HERE I COME! Swiping right like it's my job! MATCH CITY!!

I have now received not 1…but 5 unsolicited dick pics. New record!!

**Reviewer: Tony M.**      💬 **Add Comment**

**So MANY Options!**

Since becoming single, I have so many options. Ladies to the left of me, ladies to the right of me…and one lady I left. She used to text me ALL the time, wondering how I was doing, or if I needed anything. Talk about annoying. Now, nobody cares what I'm doing or how I'm doing or if I need anything. Nobody at all! It's awesome being single.

**Reviewer: Bernadette B.**      💬 **Add Comment**

**HOBBIES, HOBBIES, HOBBIES**

Learned to knit? Check. Volunteered at the local soup kitchen? Check. Started going to spin class? Check. Began building a scrapbook of my happiest memories from the past few years that don't include him? Still digging for pics and content. Get laid? Working on it.

# HINDSIGHT'S
# HALL OF MIRRORS
## A SHORT STORY

Maya's twenty-three-year marriage was fading. There was no dramatic precipitating event, just a long, slow, sad divergence. As loneliness and regret sunk in, and the future looked increasingly bleak, her thoughts turned to the beautiful boy with the long, golden hair she had lived with when she was eighteen.

She and Brad had been so profoundly in love, spending their days together in a cozy apartment, having passionate sex and wild parties. Everything had been so exciting, so full of promise, so far removed from her current life of jogging, bran muffins, and arts and crafts nights with friends.

When she entered the Time Travel Vacations Incorporated building, she gazed at the giant posters of ecstatic vacationers hugging deceased grandmothers, playing with long-dead pets, and reuniting with long-lost lovers. As she signed the forms, she noted the severe warning about penalties for committing crimes in the past. The technology didn't allow customers to change the future in any way. Once you were done mucking around as your earlier self, the timeline reverted to what it had been with no ill effects. Some early vacationers had taken the lack of consequences as a license to go on rampages, triggering the development of a new code of time-travel ethics and laws.

Maya expected to be taken to a chair and hooked up to all sorts of wires and gadgets, but instead she was brought to an empty chamber, a wide cylinder of smooth metal, its circumference unbroken once the door clanged shut behind her.

There were no flashing lights or swirling tunnels. She was just suddenly there, in the old basement suite with a young man who did not match the beautiful boy of her recollections—her Brad. His hair hung lank and greasy as he sat on the threadbare sofa, focusing intently on a television show that appeared to be nothing but car crashes. In a basement suite that smelled vaguely of mildew and unwashed feet, he turned his shockingly unbeautiful face to her and said, "Hey, babe, we're out of beer. Could you go pick some up?"

He never bought anything, never did anything, she remembered. She caught her reflection in the mirror above the sofa and was shocked to see how attractive she was. Carrying an extra thirty-five-pounds back then, she'd thought herself homely and had been so grateful to have a boyfriend. She'd believed that at any moment he might realize he could do better and toss her to the curb.